THE SCIENCE & ART
OF COACHING SERIES

MW00783523

101
DROPBACK
PASS PATTERNS

Steve Axman

ISBN: 1-58518-591-4
Library of Congress Catalog Card Number: 2001095647

Book design: Jeanne Hamilton
Diagrams: Michelle Nicholas
Cover design: Rebecca Gold
Cover photo: Joanie Komura (used by permission from the University of Washington Sports Information).

Coaches Choice
P.O. Box 1828
Monterey, CA 93942
www.coacheschoiceweb.com

DEDICATION

To all of "my boys" at
Northern Arizona University

"A great group of coaches!
A greater group of people!!!"

Robb Aikey	*Bob Lopez*
Gary Anderson	*Bronco Mendenhall*
Dino Babers	*Marty Mornhinweg*
Joe Barry	*Thurman Moore*
Bill Busch	*Brent Myers*
Charlie Dickey	*Scott Pelluer*
Kurame Dixon	*Eric Price*
Karl Dorrell	*Cliff Schwenke*
Willie Dudley	*liff Schwenke*
Bobby Hauck	*John Skadany*
Larry Kerr	*James Spurlock*
Joe Kersting	*Brian Stewart*
Steve Kragthorpe	*Kevin Sullivan*

ACKNOWLEDGMENTS

I cannot do justice to all of the many people who have taught me so much about the passing game. Very special acknowledgement to these mentors . . . Dom Anile, Homer Smith, Lindy Infante, and Mouse Davis. A special thank you to Erin Chiarelli fro her help in developing the manuscript.

PREFACE

D oes this book present ALL of the possible pass patterns a coach could utilize? ...GOODNESS, NO! However, this book does try to present the reader with a solid cross representation of as many pass pattern concepts as possible. What one must understand is that the potential combination of pass routes that make up pass patterns is almost endless. A coach can mix and match the many, many varied pass pattern concepts displayed in this book to fit the needs and desires of his own particular offense.

What this author does believe is that a coach should either mirror or mix-and-match pattern concepts that allow the quarterback to go to the "best side" depending on the pass coverage seen in front of him. Also, the timing of the pattern should utilize outlets that are timed two-steps later than the prime route(s) of the pattern. In this fashion, the quarterback can scan to outlets that are designed to come open in sync to the time it takes for him to scan to them.

CONTENTS

Arrow route connotation:	Signifies route course; or, stay on-the-move versus man coverage.
Block connotation:	Stay in and block. No route assignment.
Block-release connotation:	Check blocking assignment. If the defender does not come, release into the assigned route.
Back double-read, block-release connotation:	Back has a double-check blocking assignment. If the defenders do not come, the back releases into his assigned route. Usually associated with slide protection.
Circled "DUMP":	Dump-off route(s) for the quarterback.
Circle "I":	Signifies initial read. The quarterback takes it if it is "gimme."

DIAGRAM KEY

Circled "numbers":

①-②-③

Signifies the read progression of the quarterback.

Circled "outlet":

(Outlet)

Designates route as an outlet route.

Dotted line:

Signifies a needed route conversion (as versus a two-deep coverage); or, an alternate route action.

Long wavy line:

Signifies motion action.

Number with "S":

7$_s$

Signifies the number of steps to a route break.

Short, choppy route connotation:

Signifies a route sitting down in a zone void opening.

DIAGRAM KEY

Short, semicircular route connotation:

Signifies sitting down in a zone void opening.

Square with "H":

Signifies a "hot" route by that receiver.

Uncircled number on a QB drop:

Signifies the number of steps taken on a quarterback dropback set-up.

Uncircled number on a route:

Signifies the route depth or the route break in yards.

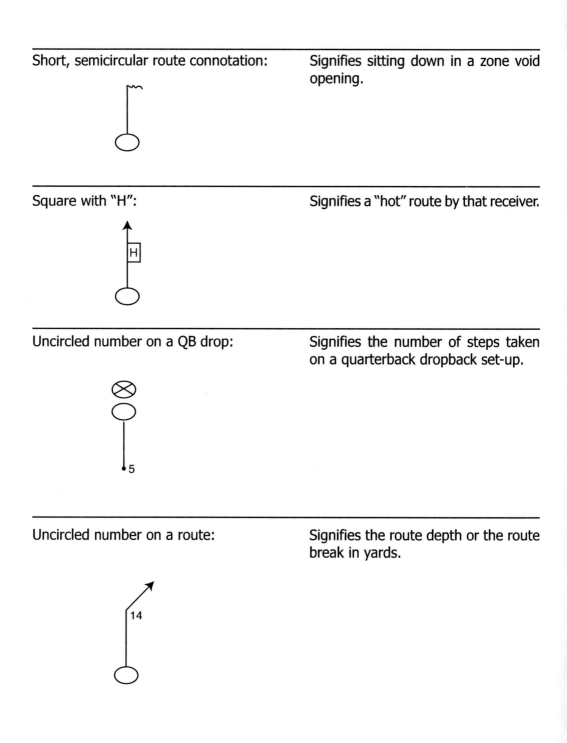

CHAPTER 1

QUICK PATTERNS

1. QUICK HITCH

Concept: Quick hitch routes to exploit soft zone and loose man coverages.

Pattern:

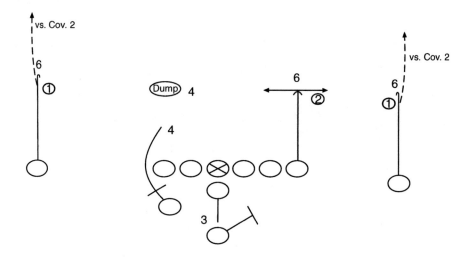

Quarterback Drop Timing: Three steps.

Key Thoughts: Wide receivers burst to sell *streak* threats. *Hitches* adjust to *fades* vs. squat or press coverages. Tight end's *quick option* and back's *dump* routes are the outlets. Quarterback takes best pre-snap read.

Alternate Pattern Application: Possible *hitch-and-go* action shown.

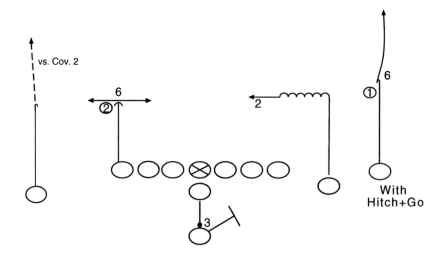

2. QUICK SPEED OUT

Concept: *Quick speed out* routes to exploit soft zone and loose man coverages.

Pattern:

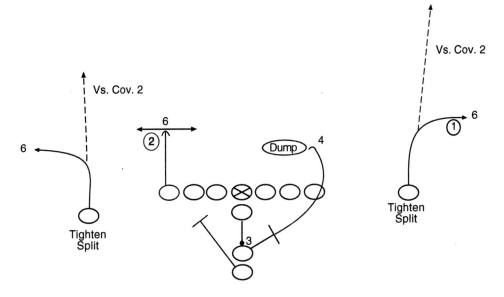

Quarterback Drop Timing: Three steps.

Key Thoughts: Wide receivers burst for two steps, rolling over on a third step, building to six yards. The *speed outs* adjust to *fades* vs. squat or press coverages. Tight end's *quick option* and back's *dump* routes are the outlets. Quarterback takes best pre-snap read.

Alternate Pattern Application: Possible *out and up* action shown.

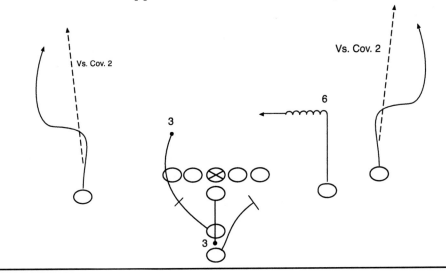

3. QUICK DOUBLE OUT

Concept: *Quick speed out* routes by inside receivers to exploit soft flat zone coverage underneath *streak clear-outs.*

Pattern:

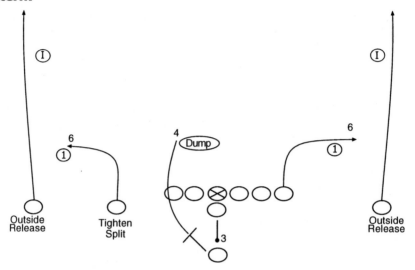

Quarterback Drop Timing: Three steps.

Key Thoughts: Wide receivers MUST outside release. Quarterback attempts to deliver quick *speed out* pass to inside receiver before he gets to the field numbers so he can knife up field vs. squatted flat zone coverage. Quarterback MUST look for *streak* hole throw. Back's *dump* route is the outlet. Quarterback takes best pre-snap read.

Alternate Pattern Application: From trips set.

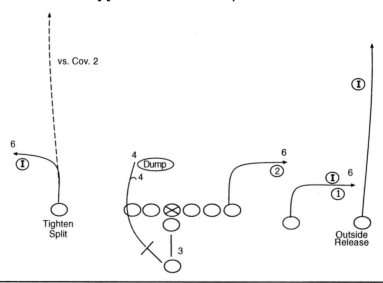

4. QUICK SLANT

Concept: *Quick slant* routes to exploit soft zone coverages to inside as well as man coverage. Best vs. single safety coverages.

Pattern:

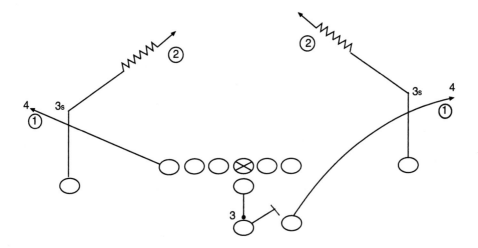

Quarterback Drop Timing: Three steps.

Key Thoughts: Tight end and weakside back must expand flatly into flat (don't build up field initially). Quarterback takes best pre-snap read to either side and looks to throw flat route until he can't. If defender drops to flat, *slant* opens. Could *fade* adjust *slants* vs. squat or press coverage.

Alternate Pattern Application: Possible *slant-go* action shown.

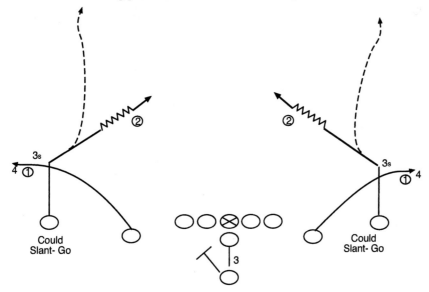

5. QUICK DOUBLE SLANT

Concept: Quick *double slant* routes to a slot formation to place a 2-on-1 isolation on a defender covering the inside *slant*. Best versus double safety coverages.

Pattern:

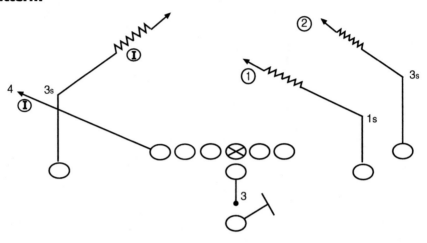

Quarterback Drop Timing: Three steps.

Key Thoughts: Quarterback reads defender covering slot. Possible quick throw to inside *slant* if defender works to outside. If defender jumps inside *slant*, a window should be open to outside *slant*. Quarterback takes best pre-snap read.

Alternate Pattern Application: From trips set.

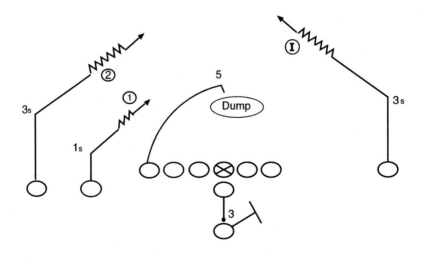

6. QUICK PIVOT

Concept: Quick outside *pivot* route action off of *double-slant action.*

Pattern:

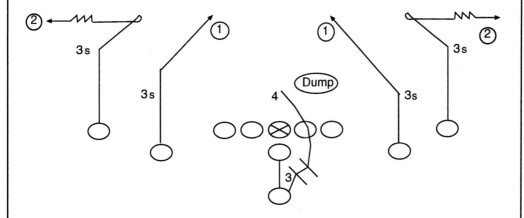

Quarterback Drop Timing: Three or quick five steps.

Key Thoughts: Quarterback initially reads inside *slants* for possible quick throw. He then works outside of corresponding inside *slant* for *pivot* throw. Back's *dump* route is the outlet. Quarterback takes best pre-snap read.

Alternate Pattern Application: Double *pivot.*

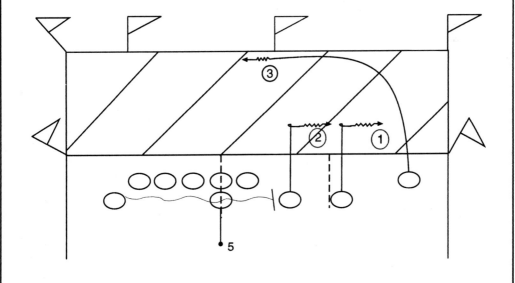

15

7. QUICK SQUARE-IN

Concept: Quick square-in route into void created by streak clear-out route.

Pattern:

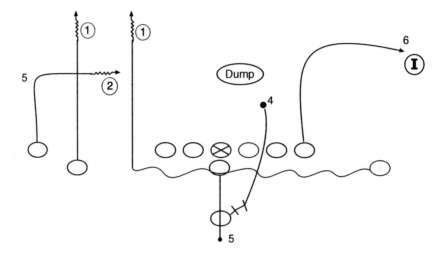

Quarterback Drop Timing: Quick five steps.

Key Thoughts: Quarterback reads *streak clear-out* routes for possible second-level throws before going to *square-in* route. *Square-in* route works zone void. Against man coverage, separate and stay on the move. Quarterback takes best pre-snap read.

Alternate Pattern Application: *Square-in* with end line options.

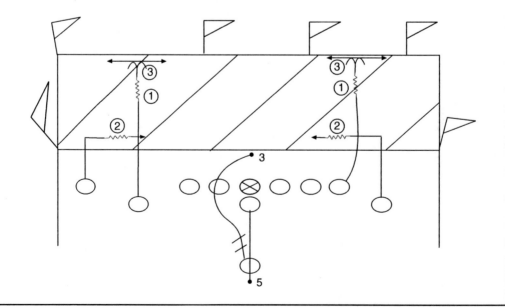

8. QUICK FADE

Concept: *Quick fade* routes to isolate on red zone/goal line man coverages (or pressed man coverages out in the field).

Pattern:

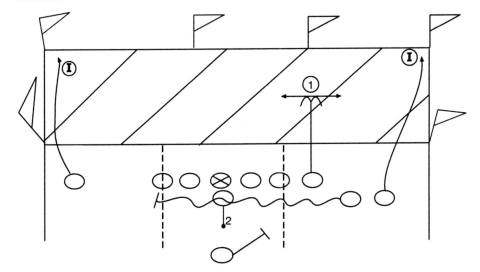

Quarterback Drop Timing: Three steps (two steps when close to goal line).

Key Thoughts: Quarterback must get the ball up quickly to allow it to drop into the corner of the end zone (two-step timing when close to the goal line). Tight end's *option route* and wing's *dump* routes are the outlets. Quarterback takes best pre-snap read.

Alternate Pattern Application:

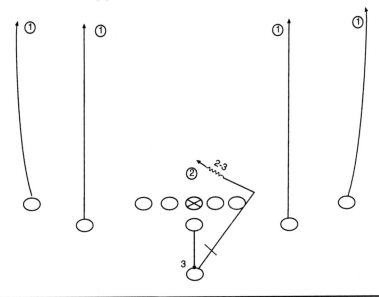

9. QUICK SMASH

Concept: Quick red zone/goal line *post-corner* isolation route by slotted receiver with *line* route by the outside receiver.

Pattern:

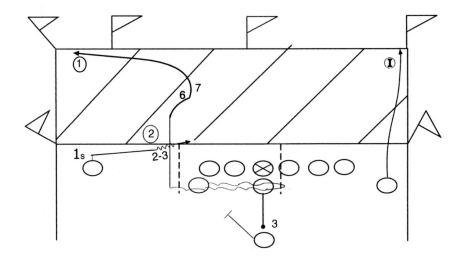

Quarterback Drop Timing: Three or quick five steps.

Key Thoughts: Isolation of the slot receiver vs. head-up or inside out man coverage. One-step *line* route is outlet. Quarterback still takes best pre-snap read.

Alternate Pattern Application: With tight end's *scat-go* route.

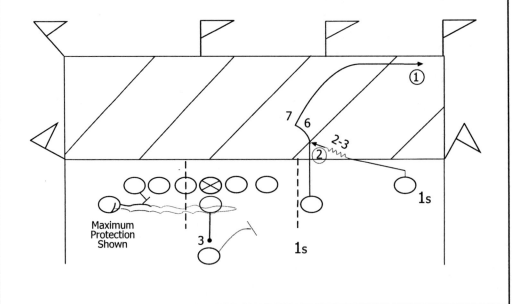

10. QUICK TRIPS POST-CORNER

Concept: Quick inside slot receiver *post-corner* isolation with two outside receiver *hitches* to hold down deep coverage.

Pattern:

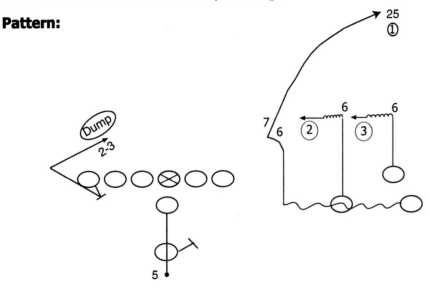

Quarterback Drop Timing: Quick five steps.

Key Thoughts: Quarterback reads deep coverage area for possible deep *quick post-corner* route isolation throw. If deep coverage is read, quarterback works down to inside *hitch* to outside *hitch* throw possibilities.

Alternate Pattern Application: With *square-ins.*

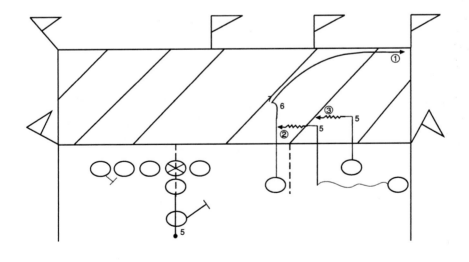

11. QUICK OPTION

Concept: Quick 1-on-1 isolation *option* route.

Pattern:

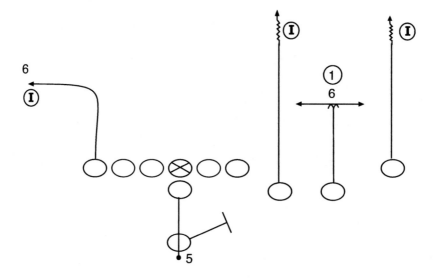

Quarterback Drop Timing: Quick five steps.

Key Thoughts: Receiver must "get open" vs. man-to-man or zone coverage. Quarterback reads *option* receiver so he can see both sides of the *option* receiver's two-way go possibility. Quarterback still takes best pre-snap read.

Alternate Pattern Application: With inside slot receiver.

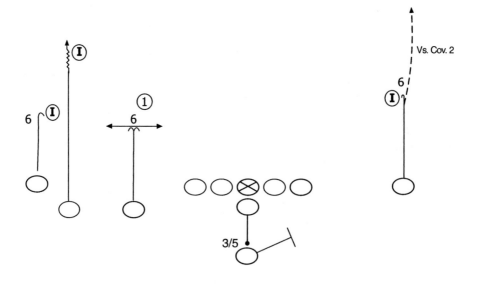

12. QUICK DRAG

Concept: *Quick drag* route underneath a *streak clear-out* route. *Drag* receiver must find zone void or separate from man-to-man coverage.

Pattern:

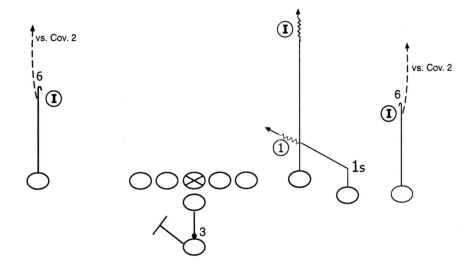

Quarterback Drop Timing: Three or quick five steps.

Key Thoughts: *Drag* receiver works zone void underneath *streak clearout*. Versus man coverage, the *drag* receiver MUST beat his man across the formation. Quarterback still takes best pre-snap read to either side.

Alternate Pattern Application: With outside trips receiver.

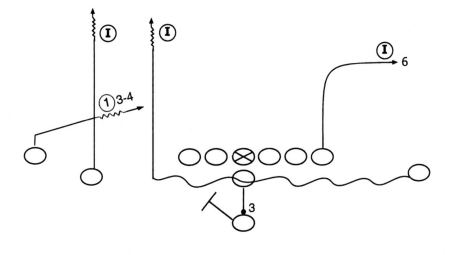

13. QUICK SCAT

Concept: *Quick flat flood* route by back with a *quick tight end stick* route. *Backside line* route serves as outlet.

Pattern:

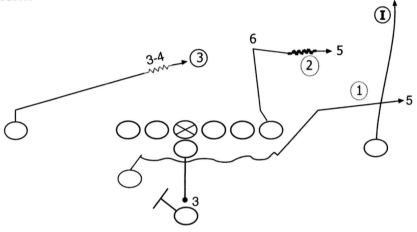

Quarterback Drop Timing: Three steps.

Key Thoughts: Quarterback looks to throw quickly to back's expansion *flat* route. If there is coverage on the *flat,* tight end's *stick* route should be open. *Line* route working backside linebacker area is the outlet.

Alternate Pattern Application: Flanker *scat* route.

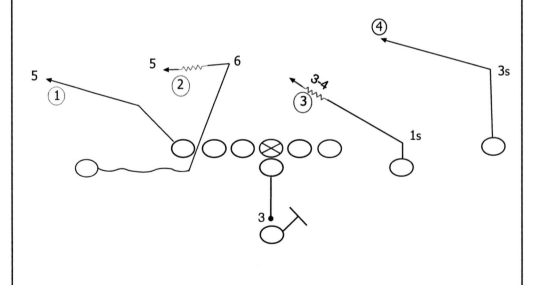

14. QUICK PICK

Concept: Quick (legal) *pick* route in which *flat* route expands over goal line as slot receiver sets (legal) stationary pick on defender covering *flat* route.

Pattern:

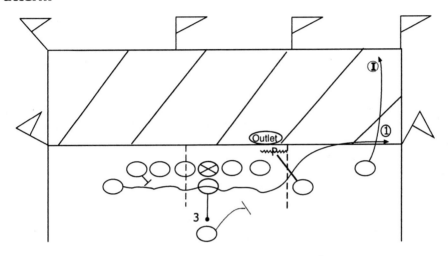

Quarterback Drop Timing: Three steps.

Key Thoughts: Slot runs a *stop hitch* type route two-to-three yards from the defender man-covering the *flat* route. Picker is a late outlet if quarterback snaps his eyes to him. *Flat* route flattens out once he crosses over the goal line. Pre-snap fade read is still a possibility.

Alternate Pattern Application: *Fade pick* route.

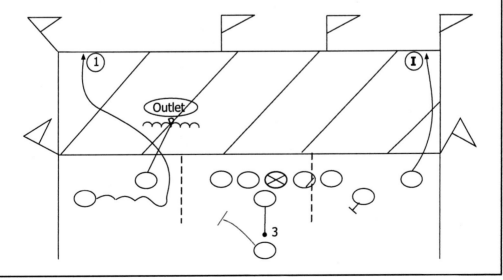

CHAPTER 2

MIRRORED DOUBLE-PRIME READ PATTERNS

15. DOUBLE OUT

Concept: Five-step, timed double *out* pattern to isolate *outs* versus soft flat zone coverage and loose man coverages.

Pattern:

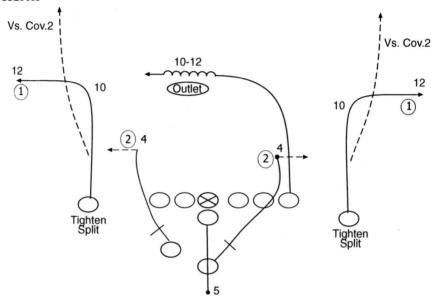

Quarterback Drop Timing: Five-step, timed plant/throw.

Key Thoughts: Quarterback MUST throw on time to *outs*. *Outs fade* adjust vs. squat or press coverage. Quarterback must be ready to go to tight end and backs as outlets.

Alternate Pattern Application: With back's *cross* action.

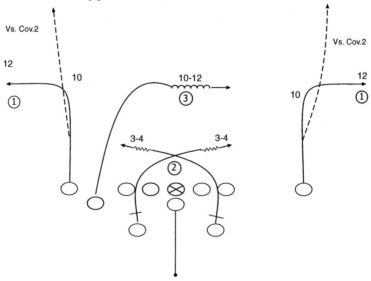

16. DOUBLE CURL

Concept: Five-step, timed double *curl* pattern to create a lateral read isolation vs. three-deep type coverages.

Pattern:

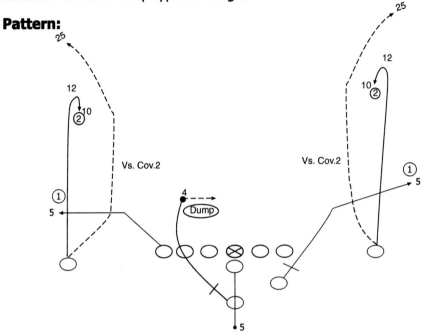

Quarterback Drop Timing: Five steps.

Key Thoughts: Quarterback thinks "throw the *flat* route" until he can't. If *flat* route is taken away, *curl* should be open. Versus cover two, *curl* route *post corner* adjusts to produce high/low read on the corner.

Alternate Pattern Application:

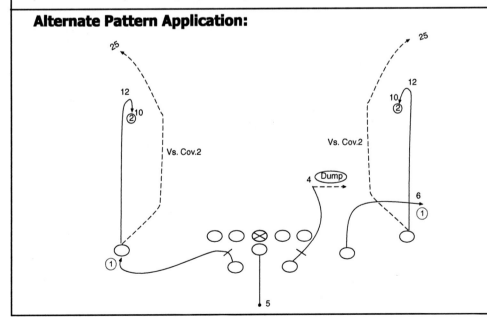

17. TRIPLE CURL

Concept: Five-step, timed triple *curl* pattern that is read inside out.

Pattern:

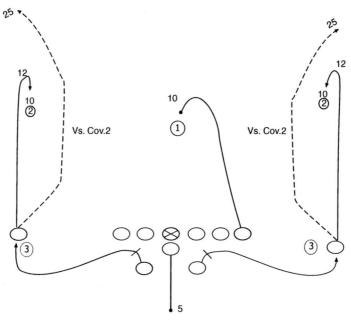

Quarterback Drop Timing: Five steps.

Key Thoughts: Quarterback reads tight end's *curl* first. If he sees "color" on the tight end, he goes to the outside *curl* to the side of that "color", then to the corresponding back's *swing* route.

Alternate Pattern Application:

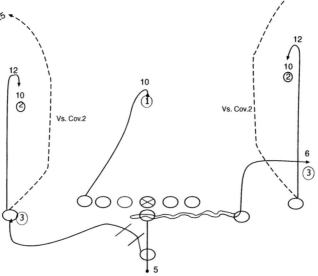

18. DOUBLE HOOK

Concept: Seven-step, timed double *hook* pattern to create a deeper lateral read isolation vs. three-deep type coverages.

Pattern:

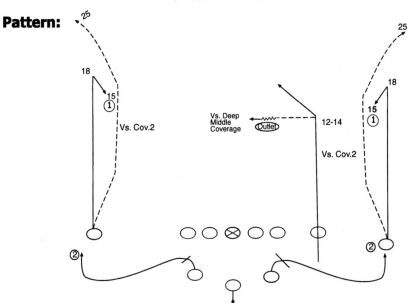

Quarterback Drop Timing: Seven steps.

Key Thoughts: Quarterback looks to *swing* routes to influence zone coverage to expand to flats so deep hooks can be thrown. Flexed tight end runs a deep *hook* as the outlet vs. deep middle coverage. Versus two-deep middle, quarterback looks to tight end's *post* break to *post-corner* adjust routes of wide receivers.

Alternate Pattern Application: With tight end's *flat* route.

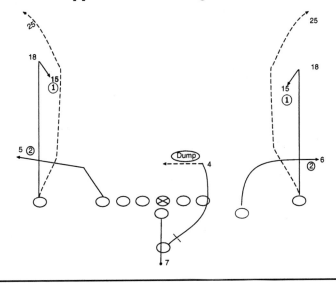

19. DOUBLE COMEBACK

Concept: Five-to-seven step, timed double *comeback* pattern to isolate *comeback outs* vs. deep zone and man coverages.

Pattern:

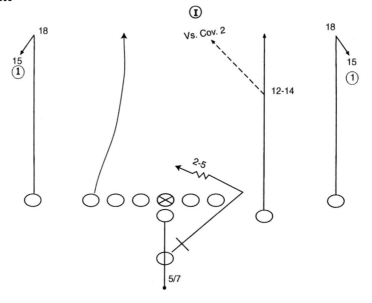

Quarterback Drop Timing: Five or seven steps.

Key Thoughts: Quarterback looks for possible 2-on-1 isolation vs. single safety, or slot *post* break vs. a two-deep middle. Cornerbacks can be used as prime routes in good 1-on-1 isolations or as outlets. Back's *delay* is outlet.

Alternate Pattern Application: With back's *fake double cross*.

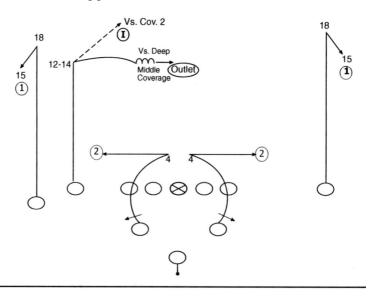

20. DOUBLE SQUARE-IN

Concept: Five-to-seven step, timed double *square-in* pattern to create inside high/low isolations.

Pattern:

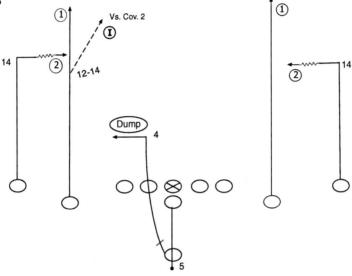

Quarterback Drop Timing: Five-to-seven steps.

Key Thoughts: Quarterback looks for possible 2-on-1 isolation vs single safety, or slot *post* break vs. a two deep middle. Quarterback then comes down to *square-ins*. *Delay* of back is outlet.

Alternate Pattern Application:

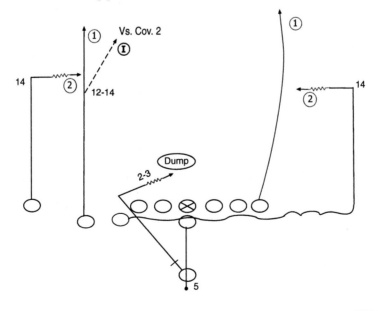

21. DOUBLE SQUARE-OUT

Concept: Five-step, timed double *square-out* pattern to create an outside high/low isolation.

Pattern:

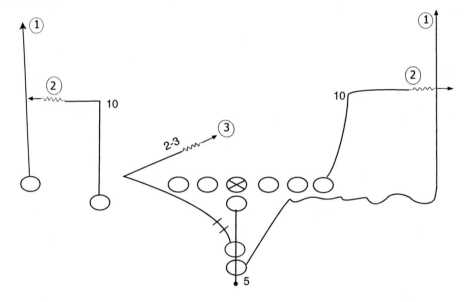

Quarterback Drop Timing: Five steps.

Key Thoughts: Quarterback looks for best high/low isolation read to the outside. Quarterback checks *streak* and comes down to *square out*. Back's *delay* is the outlet.

Alternate Pattern Application:

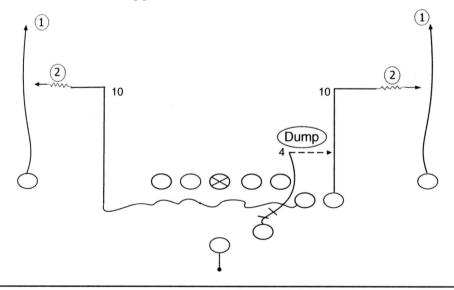

22. DOUBLE SMASH

Concept: Five-step, timed double *post-corner/smash* pattern to create outside high/low isolations.

Pattern:

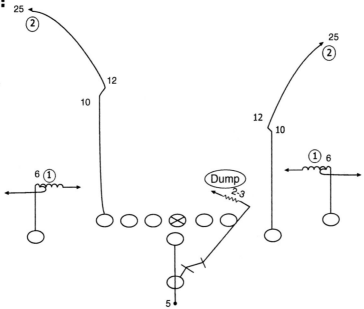

Quarterback Drop Timing: Five steps.

Key Thoughts: Quarterback looks for best high/low isolation to both sides. When in doubt, quarterback should throw low. He should never throw over the head of a retreating corner. *Smash* route MUST "get open". Back's *delay* route is the outlet.

Alternate Pattern Application: With back's *middle streak.*

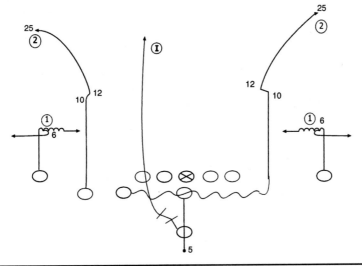

23. DOUBLE POST

Concept: Five-step, timed 2-on-1 *post* isolation pattern best used vs. a three-deep safety. Versus a two-deep coverage, *posts* adjust to squat coverage *post-corners*.

Pattern:

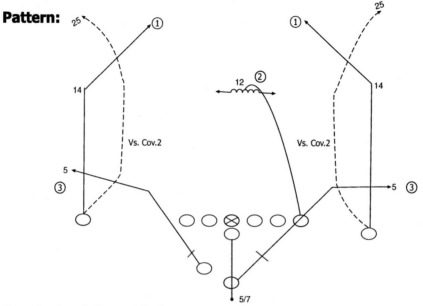

Quarterback Drop Timing: Five-to-seven steps.

Key Thoughts: Quarterback throws to post route opposite of the play of the three-deep safety. The tight end's option route becomes the outlet. If two-deep coverage, quarterback high/low reads one side or the other to throw high to the adjusted *post-corner* or low to the back's *flat* route.

Alternate Pattern Application:

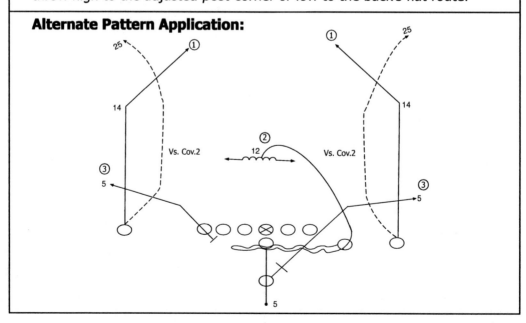

24. TWINS POST-CORNER DOUBLE POST

Concept: A seven-step, timed weak flood pattern from twins formation in an attempt to create a 3-on-2 deep isolation.

Pattern:

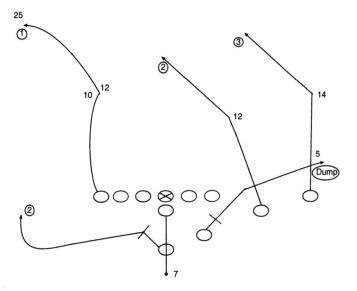

Quarterback Drop Timing: Seven steps.

Key Thoughts: Quarterback high/low reads for possible tight end *post-corner* route throw or to back's flat. If "color" appears on the *post-corner* from over the top, quarterback scans to slot's *short post* to split end's *deep post.*

Alternate Pattern Application:

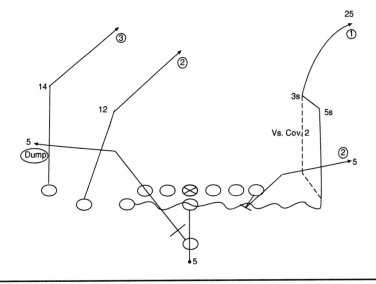

25. DOUBLE POST-CORNER

Concept: Seven- or five-step, timed double *post-corner* pattern to isolate *post-corners* vs. single coverage.

Pattern:

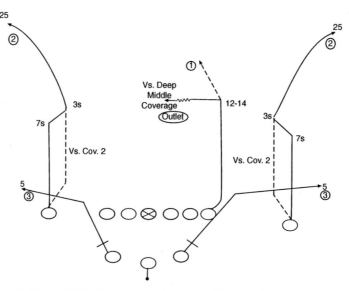

Quarterback Drop Timing: Seven steps (five if shorter *post-corners*).

Key Thoughts: Excellent red zone, man-coverage isolation routes to the outside. Quarterback reads tight end's *post* break vs. two-deep coverage before going outside to cover-two *post-corner* adjustment routes by the wide receivers.

Alternate Pattern Application:

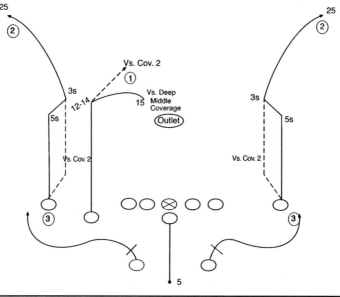

36

CHAPTER 3

STREAK PATTERNS

26. THREE STREAK

Concept: Five-step, timed triple-*streak* pattern to isolate *streaks* versus outside coverage.

Pattern:

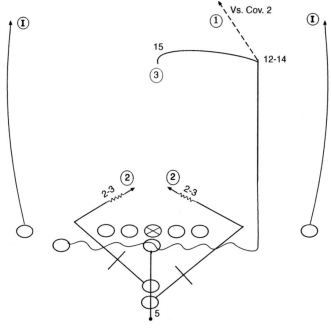

Quarterback Drop Timing: Five steps.

Key Thoughts: Quarterback looks for best 1-on-1 deep *streak* isolation by the wide receivers. Versus two-deep middle, quarterback should think slot's *post* break. *Delays* are excellent outlets.

Alternate Pattern Application:

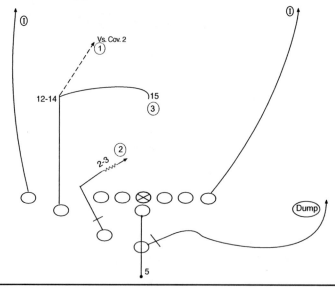

27. TIGHT END DELAY

Concept: Tight end's *delay* off five-step, timed triple-*streak* pattern isolating *streaks* versus outside coverage.

Pattern:

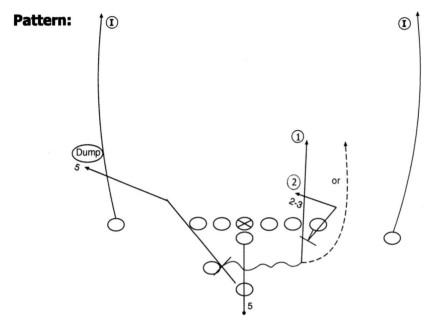

Quarterback Drop Timing: Five-to-seven steps.

Key Thoughts: Quarterback checks for possible *streak* read throw initially. He then looks for tight end *delay* route.

Alternate Pattern Application: With slot's *option*.

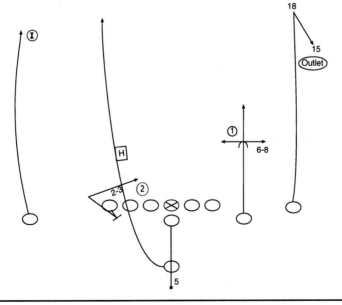

28. TIGHT END UNDER

Concept: Five-step, timed tight end's *under* route read underneath *fullback's streak clear-out* with seven-step, timed outlet.

Pattern:

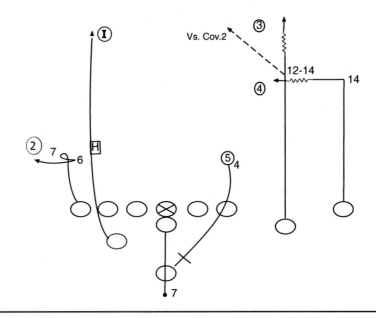

Quarterback Drop Timing: Five-to-seven steps.

Key Thoughts: *Out* route is quarterback's initial read. If clean, take it. If not, read fullback's *streak-clear* to tight end's *under* route. Split end's *post hook-up* to back's *dump* is the high/low read outlets.

Alternate Pattern Application: Tight end's *under and out*.

29. FOUR-STREAKS

Concept: Five-step, timed four-*streaks* pattern in an attempt to create a 2-on-1 inside *streak* isolation or an outside 1-on-1 *streak* isolation.

Pattern:

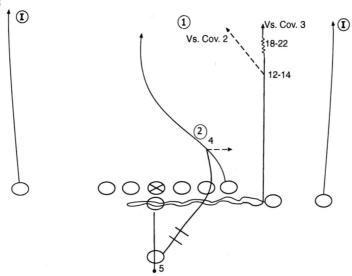

Quarterback Drop Timing: Five steps.

Key Thoughts: Quarterback looks for inside 2-on-1 *streak* isolation vs. single safety. If two-deep, read slot's *post* break. Still check for a good outside 1-on-1 *streak* isolation to outside. Back's route controls linebacker drop under *post*.

Alternate Pattern Application:

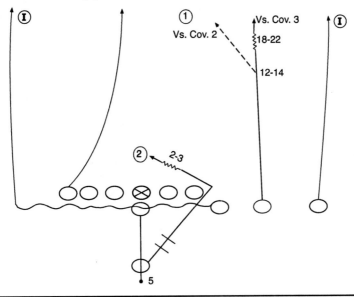

30. FOUR-STREAKS SWITCH

Concept: Seven-step, timed four-*streaks* pattern with slot/split end's *switch* action to create a delayed 2-on-1 inside streak isolation.

Pattern:

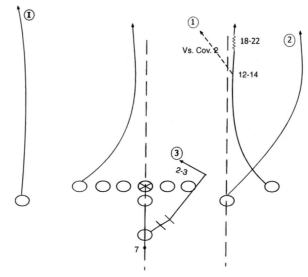

Quarterback Drop Timing: Seven steps.

Key Thoughts: Quarterback looks for inside 2-on-1 *streak* isolation vs. single safety. If two-deep, read split end's *post* break. Still check for good outside 1-on-1 flanker *streak* isolation to outside. Back's route controls linebacker drop under *post*.

Alternate Pattern Application: *Switch stop.*

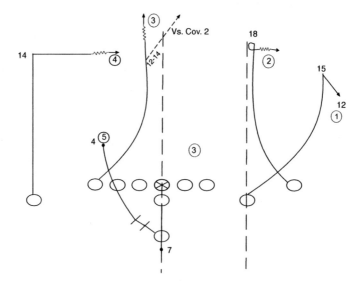

31. FIVE-STREAKS

Concept: Five-step, timed five-streaks pattern to attack four-deep coverage in an attempt to create an inside 3-on-2 isolation.

Pattern:

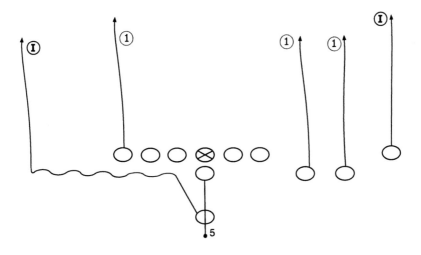

Quarterback Drop Timing: Five steps.

Key Thoughts: Quarterback looks for inside 3-on-2 *streak* isolation vs. a two-deep safety look. Still could take a good outside 1-on-1 *streak* isolation.

Alternate Pattern Application:

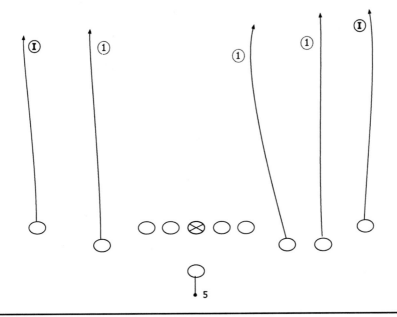

CHAPTER 4

SINGLE PRIME READ PATTERNS

32. SINGLE OUT

Concept: Five-step, timed lateral read *out* pattern with seven-step, timed backside outlet.

Pattern:

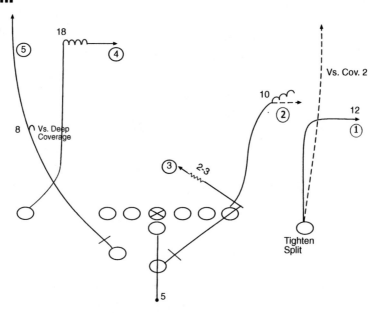

Quarterback Drop Timing: Five steps.

Key Thoughts: Lateral read of a cover-three strong safety. Versus press man, quarterback thinks tight end's man break. Versus cover-two, look for tight end in alley. Scan to backside for outlet.

Alternate Pattern Application:

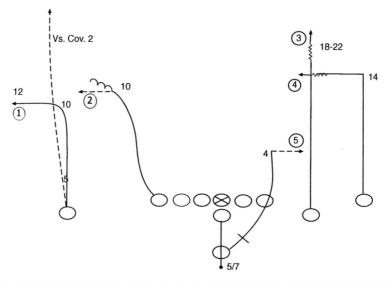

33. SINGLE CURL-FLANKER

Concept: Five-step, timed lateral read *curl* pattern with a *post* initial read route backside.

Pattern:

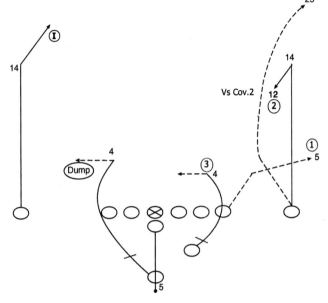

Quarterback Drop Timing: Five steps.

Key Thoughts: Quarterback takes the initial read of the split end's *post* route, if there. Quarterback thinks "throw *flat* route" until he can't. If *flat* route is taken away, *curl* should be open. Versus cover-two route *post-corner* adjusts to produce high/low isolation read on corner. The fullback's *dump* route is the outlet.

Alternate Pattern Application:

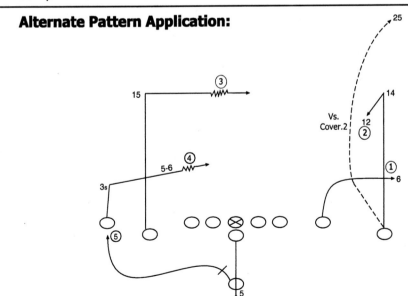

34. TIGHT END/FLANKER SQUARE IN

Concept: Seven-step, timed inside-out *scan* pattern with a *post* initial read route backside.

Pattern:

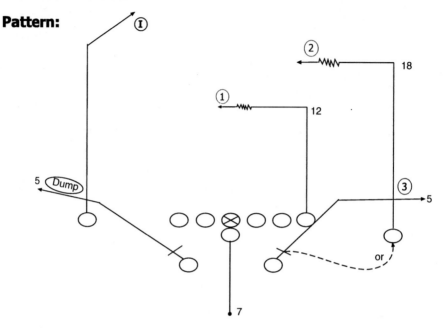

Quarterback Drop Timing: Seven steps.

Key Thoughts: Quarterback takes the initial read of the split end's *post* route, if there. Quarterback then reads tight end's *cross* route to flanker's *dig* route to back's *flat*.

Alternate Pattern Application: From trips set.

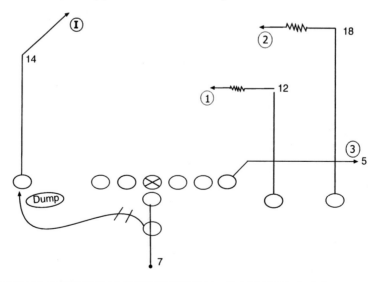

35. FLANKER/TIGHT END SQUARE IN WITH F OPTION

Concept: Seven-step, timed inside-out *scan* pattern with split end's *post* initial read route.

Pattern:

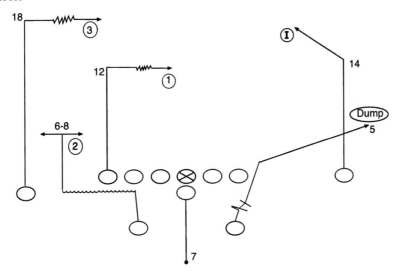

Quarterback Drop Timing: Seven steps.

Key Thoughts: Quarterback takes the initial read route of the split end's *post*, if there. Quarterback then reads tight end's *cross* route to flanker's *dig* route to fullback's *option*.

Alternate Pattern Application: With slot's *slant pivot* and *scissors*.

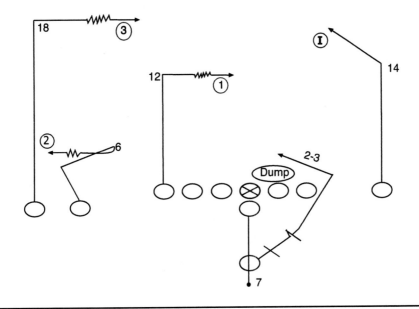

36. SPLIT END DIG

Concept: Seven-step, timed high/low read on the weakside inside linebacker with a *post* initial read route backside.

Pattern:

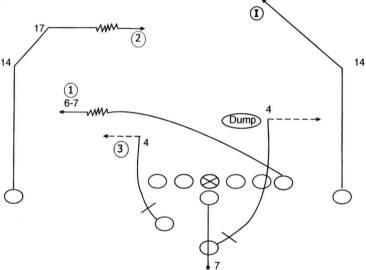

Quarterback Drop Timing: Seven-steps.

Key Thoughts: Quarterback takes the initial read of flanker's *post* route, if there. Quarterback then checks tight end's *shallow* before high/low reading the weak inside linebacker for split end's *dig* route or back's *dump*.

Alternate Pattern Application: Flanker's *dig* with fullback's *scissor*.

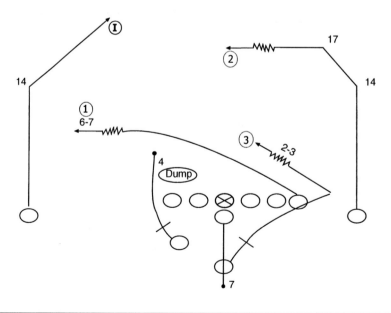

37. SINGLE CURL-SPLIT END

Concept: Five-step, timed lateral read *curl* pattern with seven-step, timed outlet.

Pattern:

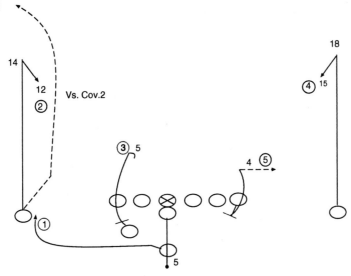

Quarterback Drop Timing: Five steps.

Key Thoughts: Quarterback thinks "throw *swing* route" until he can't. If *swing* route is taken away, *curl* should be open. Versus cover-two *curl* route, *post-corner* adjusts to produce a high/low isolation read on corner. The flanker's *hook* and the tight end's *dump* route combination backside are the outlets.

Alternate Pattern Application: With fullback's *option.*

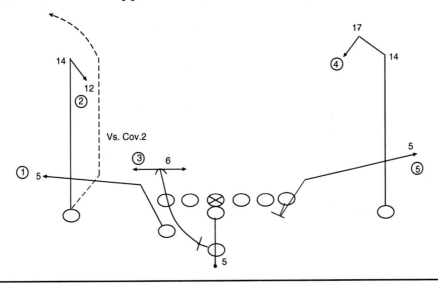

38. SINGLE POST FLANKER/TIGHT END WHEEL

Concept: Five-step, timed *post* to seven-step, timed *wheel* isolation vs. man and three-deep zone coverages.

Pattern:

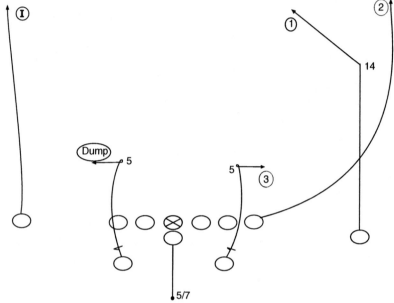

Quarterback Drop Timing: Five-to-seven steps.

Key Thoughts: Quarterback reads *post* to tight end's *wheel* to back's *pivot-out* outlets. Excellent red zone pattern.

Alternate Pattern Application: Unbalanced double *post wheel.*

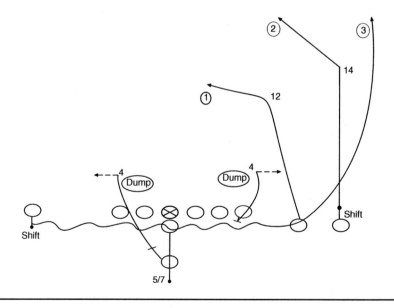

39. SINGLE POST-SPLIT END

Concept: Five-step, timed *post* isolation vs. cover-three type coverages with a seven-step, timed outlet.

Pattern:

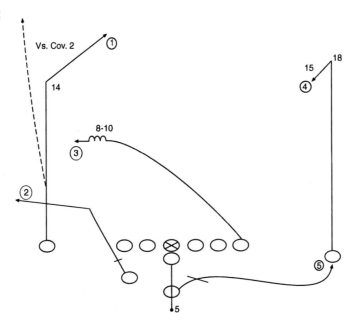

Quarterback Drop Timing: Five steps.

Key Thoughts: Quarterback looks for a good initial *post* throw (depending on the coverage), then throws flat to tight end's *over* route. Versus squatted coverage, split end's *fade* adjusts to produce a high/low read on the corner.

Alternate Pattern Application: With tailback *delay*.

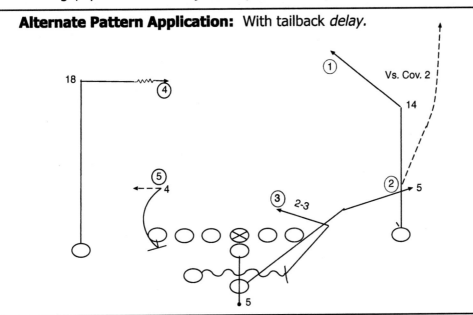

40. SINGLE SQUARE OUT

Concept: Five-step, timed *square-out* pattern to create an outside high/ low isolation with a backside seven-step, timed outlet.

Pattern:

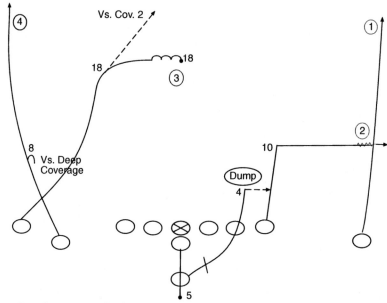

Quarterback Drop Timing: Five steps.

Key Thoughts: Quarterback checks *streak* and comes down to *square-out*. Outlet is flanker's *hook* to tight end's *around* route to back's *dump*.

Alternate Pattern Application:

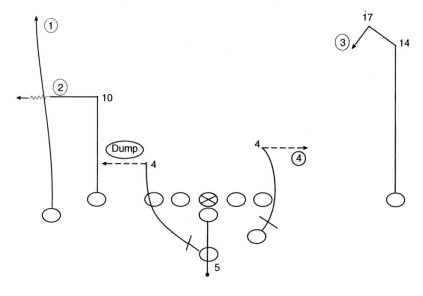

41. SPLIT END SQUARE IN—SLOT SQUARE OUT

Concept: Five-step, timed lateral read with a tight end's *post* initial read route.

Pattern:

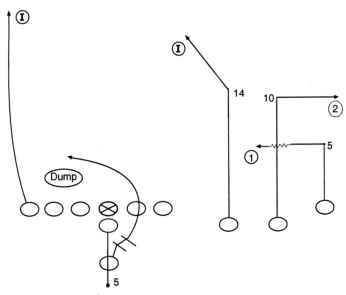

Quarterback Drop Timing: Five steps.

Key Thoughts: Quarterback takes the initial read route of the slot's *post* route, if there. Quarterback then inside-out reads the flanker's *short square-in* to the flanker-slot *square-out*. The back's *dump* route serves as the outlet.

Alternate Pattern Application: Split end's *square in*; slot's *square out*.

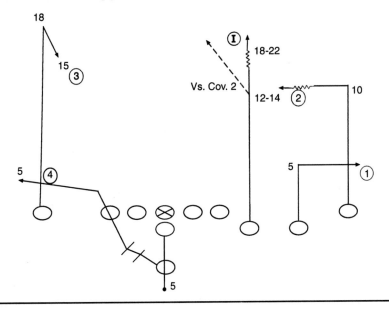

42. SLOT SQUARE OUT—SPLIT END SHALLOW

Concept: Three-to-five step, timed lateral read with a *post* initial read route backside.

Pattern:

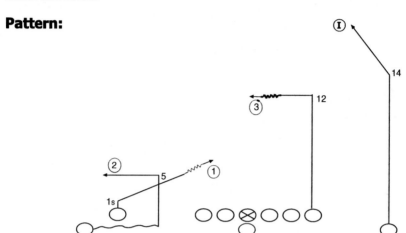

Quarterback Drop Timing: Three-to-five steps.

Key Thoughts: Quarterback takes the initial read route of the flanker's *post* route, if there. Quarterback then reads split end's *shallow* route (possible quick throw) to slot's quick *square-out*. The tight end's *cross* route is the outlet.

Alternate Pattern Application: Slot's *square-in*; tight end's *flag*.

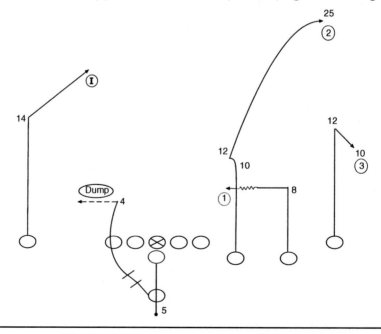

43. SINGLE SMASH

Concept: Seven-step, timed *post-corner/smash* pattern isolation with a backside seven-step, timed outlet.

Pattern:

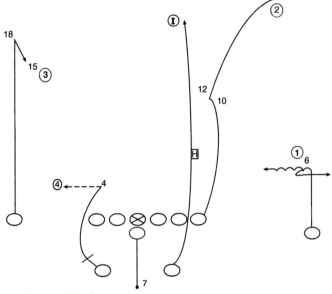

Quarterback Drop Timing: Seven steps.

Key Thoughts: Quarterback high/low reads. When in doubt, throw low. Never throw over the head of a retreating defender. *Smash* route MUST "get open".

Alternate Pattern Application: With wing motion.

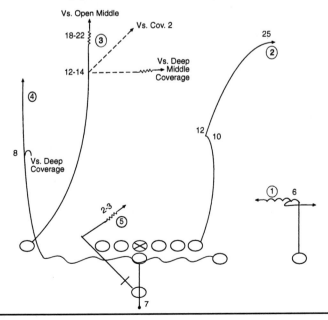

44. SINGLE POST-CORNER

Concept: Seven-step, timed *post-corner* pattern to isolate *post-corner* vs. single coverage with a backside seven-step, timed outlet.

Pattern:

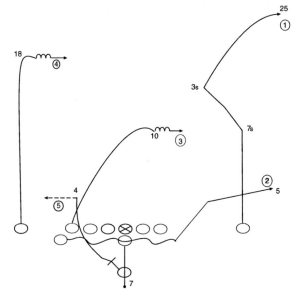

Quarterback Drop Timing: Seven steps.

Key Thoughts: Quarterback high/low reads. When in doubt, throw low. Never throw over the head of a retreating defender. Scan to backside to tight end's *middle hook-up* to flanker's *hook*. Back's *dump* is the outlet.

Alternate Pattern Application:

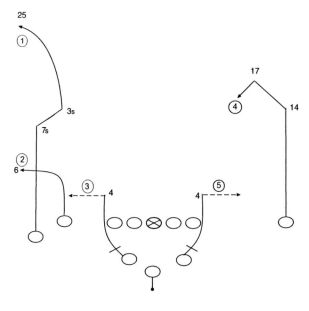

45. SPLIT END POST CORNER/FLANKER DIG

Concept: Seven-step, timed *post-corner* with *dig* tight end's *clear* outlet route combination backside.

Pattern:

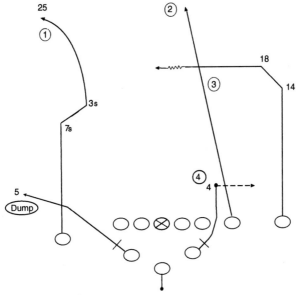

Quarterback Drop Timing: Seven steps.

Key Thoughts: Quarterback initially checks *post-corner* hole for *post-corner* throw. Quarterback then checks tight end's *clear* route deep to flanker's *dig* to back's *dump*.

Alternate Pattern Application: Flanker's *post-corner*; split end's *dig*.

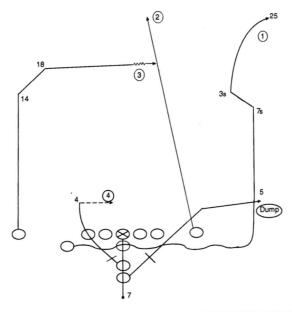

46. SINGLE STREAK—FLANKER

Concept: Five-step, timed *streak* pattern to isolate *streak* vs. single coverage.

Pattern:

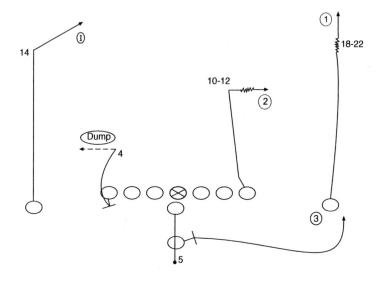

Quarterback Drop Timing: Five steps.

Key Thoughts: Quarterback isolates on single 1-on-1 deep *streak* isolation. Quarterback looks for hole throw vs. two-deep. If *streak* looks poor, quarterback scans to tight end's *out* to back's *swing*.

Alternate Pattern Application: With tight end *flood*.

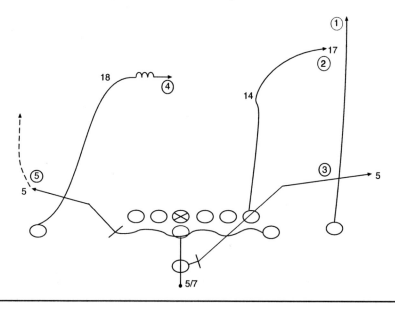

47. SINGLE STREAK—SPLIT END

Concept: Five-step, timed *streak* pattern to isolate *streak* vs. single coverage with a backside seven-step, timed outlet.

Pattern:

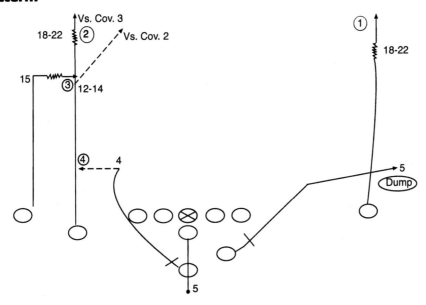

Quarterback Drop Timing: Five steps.

Key Thoughts: Quarterback isolates on single 1-on-1 deep *streak* isolation. Quarterback looks for hole throw vs. two-deep. Backside outlet read is slot's *streak* (*post* vs. two-deep) to flanker's *dig* to backs' *dump*.

Alternate Pattern Application: With tight end's *layered flood*.

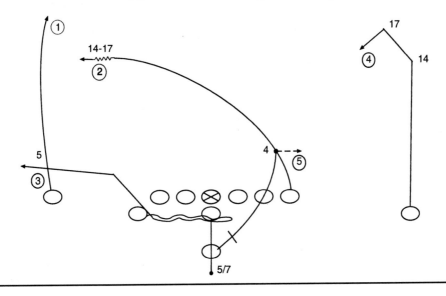

CHAPTER 5

OPTION PATTERNS

48. TIGHT END OPTION

Concept: Five-step, timed tight end's *option* route isolation after an initial read of the flanker's *speed-out* route with a seven-step, timed outlet to the backside.

Pattern:

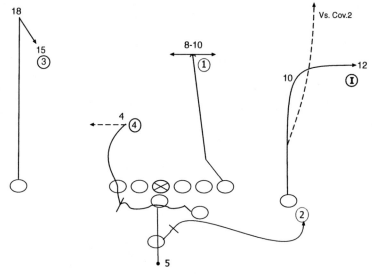

Quarterback Drop Timing: Five steps.

Key Thoughts: Quarterback takes out, if clearly there. Otherwise, quarterback reads tight end's *option* route to enable him to see to both sides of the tight end's two-way, go action. *Hook/dump* outlet is to the backside.

Alternate Pattern Application: Outside tight end's *option.*

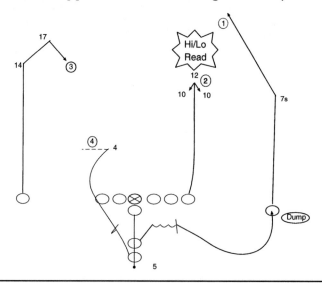

49. FULLBACK OPTION

Concept: Five-step, timed strong side fullback's *option* route isolation with a seven-step, timed outlet to the backside.

Pattern:

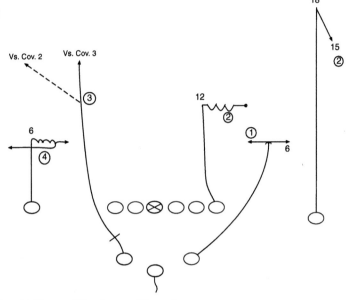

Quarterback Drop Timing: Five steps.

Key Thoughts: Quarterback reads fullback's *option* route to enable him to see both sides of the fullback's two-way, go action. The quarterback goes to the flanker's out route if he sees "color" on the *option* from the outside and to the tight end if from the inside. The tailback/split end's *smash* combination is the outlet.

Alternate Pattern Application: With wing's *option*.

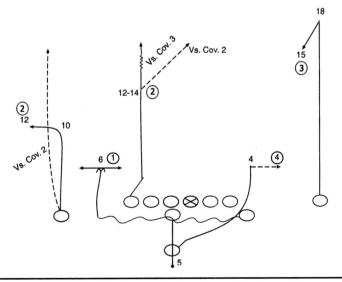

50. HALFBACK OPTION

Concept: Five-step, timed weakside halfback's *option* route isolation after an initial read of the split end's *rollaway* route with a seven-step, timed outlet to the backside.

Pattern:

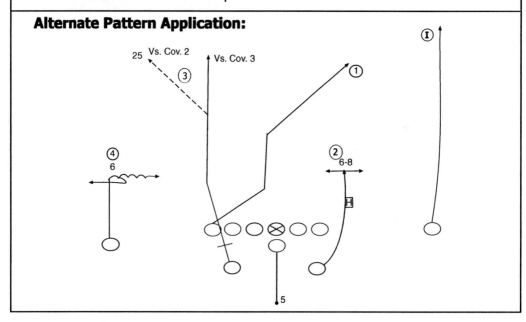

Vs. Cov. 2

Quarterback Drop Timing: Five steps.

Key Thoughts: Quarterback takes *rollaway,* if clearly there. Otherwise, quarterback reads halfback's *option* route to enable him to see to both sides of the halfback's two-way, go action. The flanker's *hook* to the tight end's *around* route to fullback's *dump* is the outlet.

Alternate Pattern Application:

51. SLOT OPTION

Concept: Five-step, timed slot's *option* route isolation in between a *speed out* and a *dump* route with a seven-step, timed outlet to the backside.

Pattern:

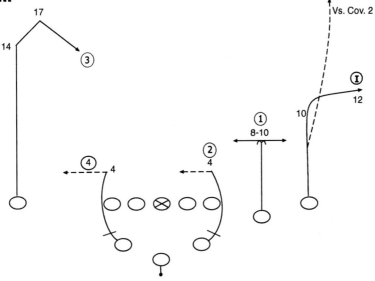

Quarterback Drop Timing: Five steps.

Key Thoughts: Quarterback reads slot's option route for 1-on-1 isolation. If double coverage appears, quarterback goes opposite double-coverage "color" to throw to speed out or dump. Backside outlet is hook/dump combination by split end and halfback.

Alternate Pattern Application:

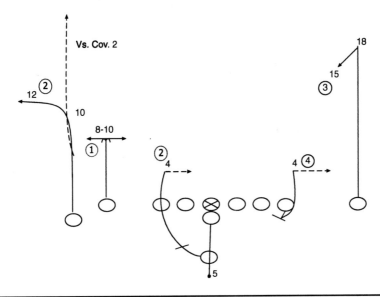

52. SPLIT END OPTION

Concept: Five-step, timed split end's *option* route isolation as back route tries to influence a bumping zone coverage to the outside to produce a good split end *option* isolation action with a seven-step, timed outlet to the backside.

Pattern:

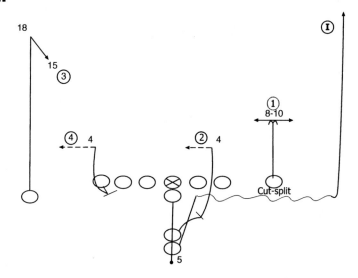

Quarterback Drop Timing: Five steps.

Key Thoughts: Back motion attempts to bump zone coverage to the outside to force split end's *option* isolation versus (hopefully) linebackers. Backside outlet is *hook/dump* outlet combination of flanker and tight end.

Alternate Pattern Application:

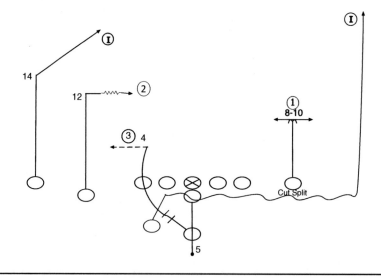

53. DOUBLE OPTION

Concept: Five-step, timed double *option* route isolations with *rollaway* initial reads to both sides.

Pattern:

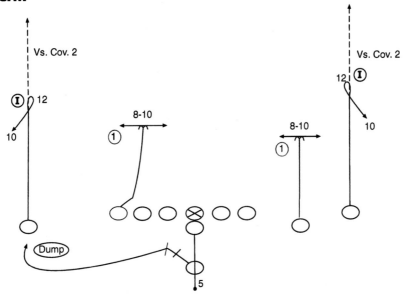

Quarterback Drop Timing: Five steps.

Key Thoughts: Quarterback takes *rollaway* to either side, if clearly there. Otherwise, quarterback takes the *option* with the best chance of 1-on-1 coverage.

Alternate Pattern Application:

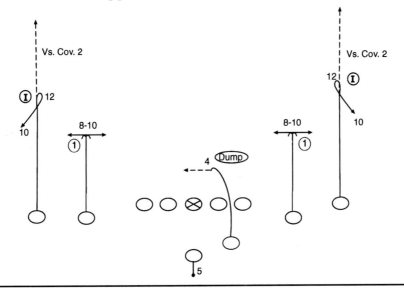

CHAPTER 6

ISOLATION PATTERNS

54. SPLIT END ROLLAWAY ISOLATION

Concept: Five-step, timed *rollaway* isolation route with quarterback scanning back to outlets working into the quarterback's scan vision and a backside *post* initial read route.

Pattern:

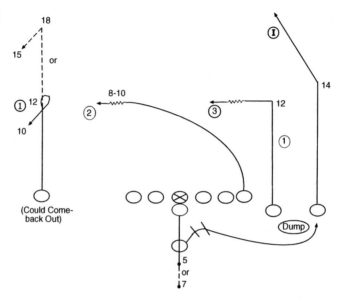

Quarterback Drop Timing: Five steps.

Key Thoughts: Quarterback takes the initial read of the flanker's *post* route if there. Quarterback reads the split end's *rollaway* route and then scans backside to the tight end's *over* route to the slot's *cross*. The back's *swing* serves as the dump-off outlet.

Alternate Pattern Application:

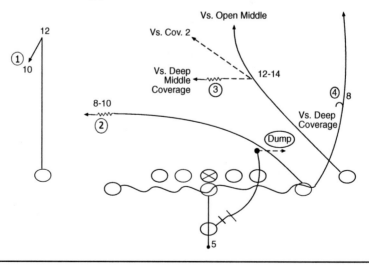

55. FLANKER ROLLAWAY ISOLTION

Concept: Five-step, timed rollaway isolation route with quarterback scanning back to outlets working into the quarterback's scan vision.

Pattern:

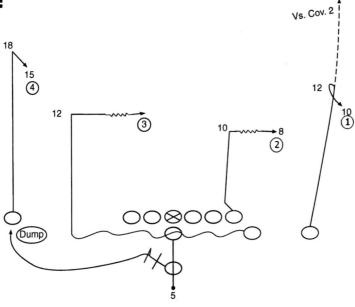

Quarterback Drop Timing: Five steps.

Key Thoughts: Quarterback reads the flanker's *rollaway* route and then scans backside to the tight end's *scat-out* route to the wing-slot's *cross* route to the split end's *hook*.

Alternate Pattern Application:

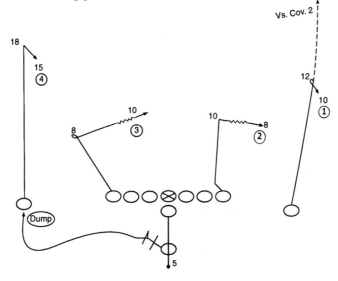

56. SPLIT END POST CORNER ISOLATION

Concept: Seven-step, timed high/low read *post-corner* isolation route with quarterback scanning back to outlets working into the quarterback's scan vision.

Pattern:

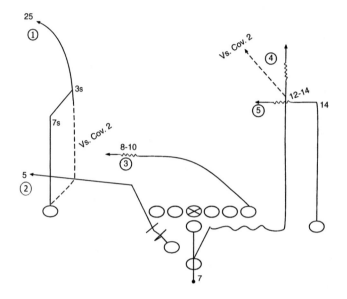

Quarterback Drop Timing: Seven steps.

Key Thoughts: Quarterback high/low reads the *post-corner* hole. If the corner gets under the *post-corner*, the quarterback throws to the back's *flat* route. The quarterback scans back to the tight end's *cross* route to the fullback's *post* route to the flanker's *square-in*.

Alternate Pattern Application:

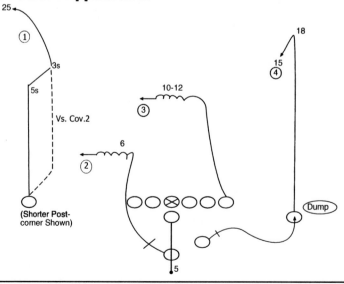

57. SPLIT END POST/HOOK-UP READ ISOLATION

Concept: Five-to-seven step, timed *post/hook-up* isolation route read with quarterback scanning back to outlets working into the quarterback's scan vision.

Pattern:

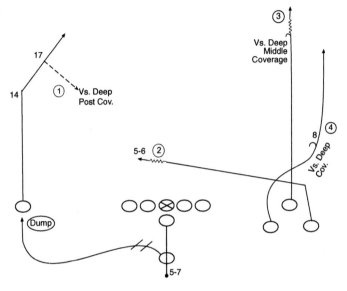

Quarterback Drop Timing: Five-to-seven steps.

Key Thoughts: Quarterback looks to throw a five-step, timed *post* route or a seven-step, timed *post/hook-up* route depending on the *post* hole coverage. Quarterback then scans back to flanker's *shallow* route to tight end's *streak/hook-up* route to slot's *wheel/hook-up*.

Alternate Pattern Application:

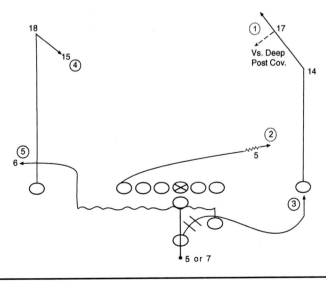

58. SPLIT END STREAK ISOLATION

Concept: Five-step, timed *streak* isolation route read with quarterback scanning back to outlets working into the quarterback's scan vision.

Pattern:

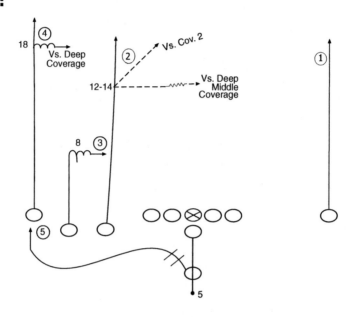

Quarterback Drop Timing: Five steps.

Key Thoughts: Quarterback looks to throw a five-step, timed *streak* isolation route. Quarterback then scans back to inside slot's *streak/hook-up* route to the outside-slot's *hitch* route to the flanker's *streak/hook-up*.

Alternate Pattern Application: *Z pump (lift-and-go)* isolation.

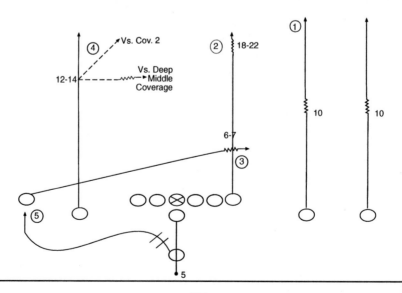

59. FLANKER HOOK-AND-GO ISOLATION

Concept: Five-step, timed *hook-and-go* isolation route with a backside *post* initial read route.

Pattern:

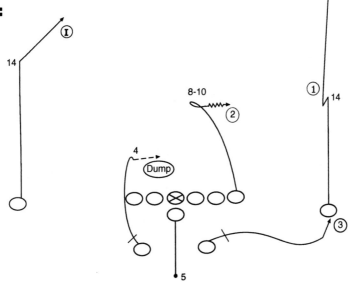

Quarterback Drop Timing: Five steps.

Key Thoughts: Quarterback takes the initial read of the split end's *post* route, if there. Quarterback reads flanker's *hook-and-go* route progressing to the tight end's *pivot out* route to the fullback's *swing*.

Alternate Pattern Application: Split end's *out-and-up* isolation.

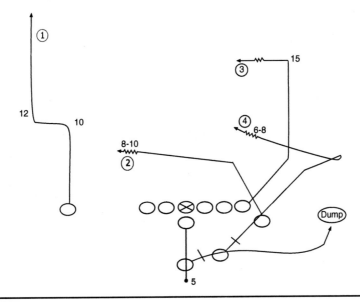

60. TIGHT END POST-CORNER ISOLATION

Concept: Five-step, timed tight end *post-corner* isolation with quarterback scanning back to outlets working into the quarterback's scan vision.

Pattern:

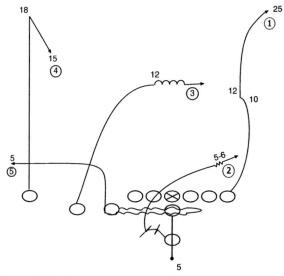

Quarterback Drop Timing: Five steps.

Key Thoughts: Quarterback reads the tight end's *post-corner* route and then scans backside to the back's *shallow* route to the flanker-slot's *middle hook* to the split end's *hook*.

Alternate Pattern Application: Tight end *comeback* or *square-out* isolation.

61. SLOT ISOLATION READ

Concept: Five-step, timed slot's *post/post-corner* isolation with the quarterback coming down to a *smash* route or scanning backside to a *middle shallow* according to coverage.

Pattern:

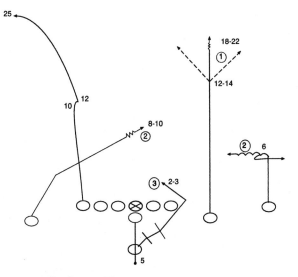

Quarterback Drop Timing: Five steps.

Key Thoughts: Slot breaks into *post*, *streak* or *post-corner* opposite alignment positioning of safety. Versus three-deep safety, run *streak-throttle*. Versus two-deep safety, run *post* if aligned head up to outside. If safety is inside, run *post-corner*. Back's *dump* route is the outlet.

Alternate Pattern Application: Y read.

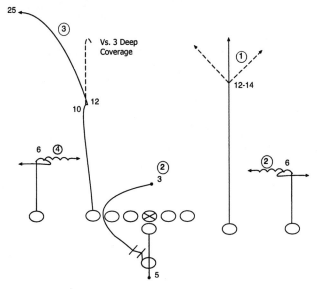

CHAPTER 7

SCAT PATTERNS

62. SCAT

Concept: Five-step, timed lateral read of back's *flat* route to tight end's *scat-out* route with seven-step, timed backside outlet.

Pattern:

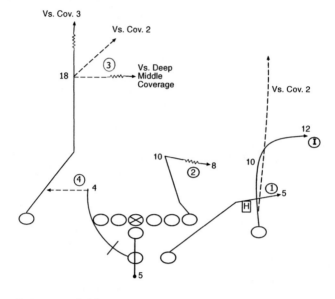

Quarterback Drop Timing: Five steps.

Key Thoughts: Quarterback takes initial read of flanker's *speed-out,* if clearly there. Otherwise, quarterback reads back's *flat* route to tight end's *scat-out.* Backside outlet is *hook/dump* combination of split end and back.

Alternate Pattern Application: With wing motion.

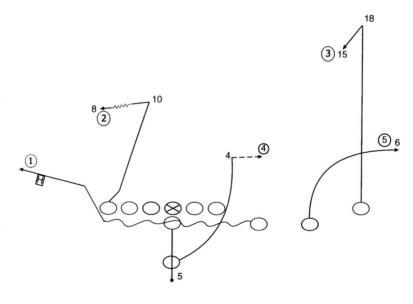

63. SCAT CROSS

Concept: Five-step, timed crossing read of tight end's *scat-out* and back's *scissor* route with seven-step, timed backside outlet.

Pattern:

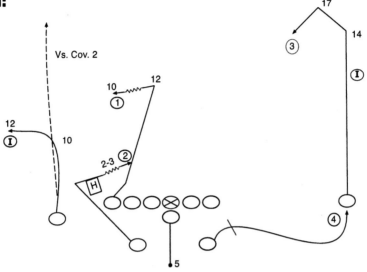

Quarterback Drop Timing: Five steps.

Key Thoughts: Quarterback takes initial read of flanker's *speed-out* route, if clearly there. Otherwise, quarterback reads tight end's *scat-out* route to back's *scissor*. Backside outlet is *hook/swing* combination of split end and back.

Alternate Pattern Application: With *scat-go* action.

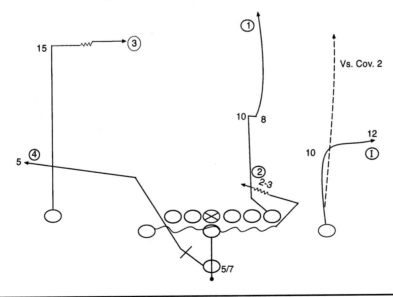

64. SCAT CROSS-FOLLOW

Concept: Five-step, timed tight end's *cross* with back's *scissor follow* route with initial read routes to both sides.

Pattern:

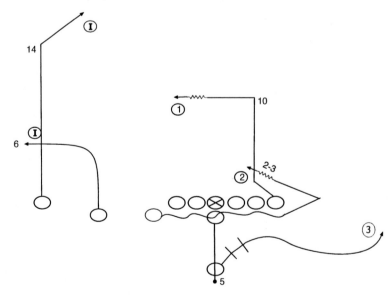

Vs. Cov. 2

Quarterback Drop Timing: Five steps.

Key Thoughts: Quarterback takes the initial read of either the flanker's *short comeback-out* or the split end's *post*, if there. Quarterback then reads back's *flat* route to tight end's *cross* route to back's *scissor*.

Alternate Pattern Application: With wing.

CHAPTER 8

SHALLOW PATTERNS

65. SPLIT END SHALLOW TIGHT END CROSS

Concept: Seven-step, timed crossing pattern with a *post* initial read route front-side.

Pattern:

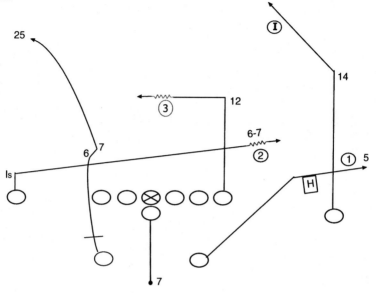

Quarterback Drop Timing: Seven steps.

Key Thoughts: Quarterback takes the initial read of the flanker's *post* route, if there. Quarterback then reads fullback's *flat* route to split end's *shallow* route to tight end's *cross*. The fullback's *flat* route can act as the dump-off route.

Alternate Pattern Application: Flanker-slot motion.

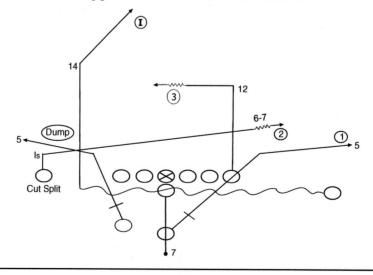

66. SLOT SHALLOW TIGHT END CROSS

Concept: Seven-step, timed crossing pattern with a *post* initial read route backside.

Pattern:

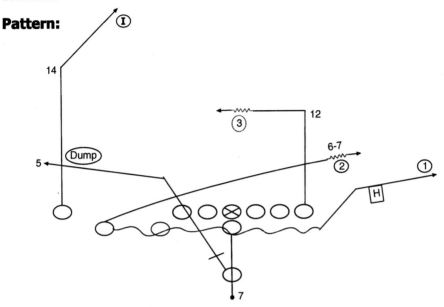

Quarterback Drop Timing: Seven steps.

Key Thoughts: Quarterback takes the initial read of the split end's *post*, if there. Quarterback then reads wing's *flat* route to slot's *shallow* route to tight end's *cross*. The fullback's *flat* route can act as the dump-off route.

Alternate Pattern Application: From wing slot motion.

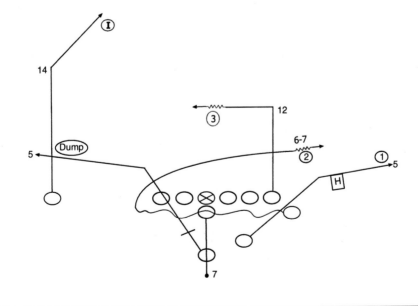

67. TIGHT END SHALLOW SLOT CROSS

Concept: Seven-step, timed crossing pattern with a *post* initial read route backside.

Pattern:

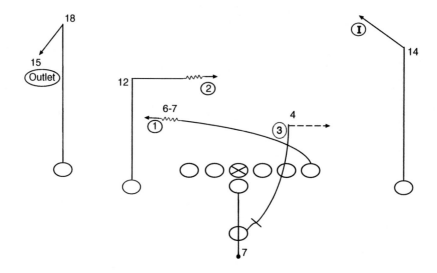

Quarterback Drop Timing: Seven steps.

Key Thoughts: Quarterback takes the initial read of the flanker's *post* route, if there. Quarterback then reads tight end's *shallow* route to slot's *cross* route to back's *dump*.

Alternate Pattern Application: Tight end *shallow* with double *post*.

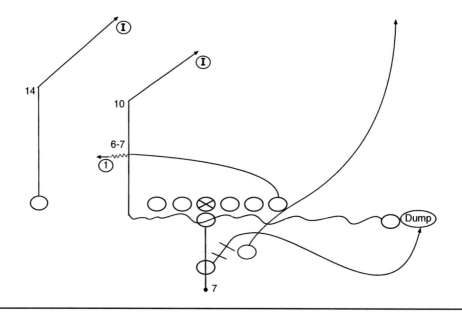

68. TIGHT END SHALLOW SPLIT END CROSS

Concept: Seven-step, timed crossing pattern with *post* initial read route backside.

Pattern:

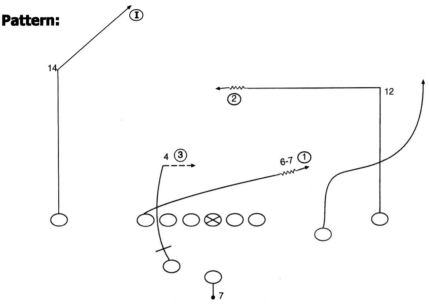

Quarterback Drop Timing: Seven steps.

Key Thoughts: Quarterback takes the initial read of the flanker's *post* route, if there. Quarterback then reads tight end's *shallow* route to split end's *cross* route to back's *dump*.

Alternate Pattern Application: From double-tight end, one-back set.

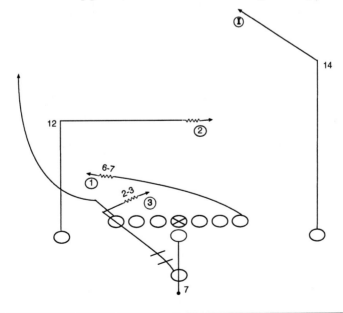

69. FLANKER SHALLOW SPLIT END CROSS

Concept: Seven-step, timed crossing pattern with tight end's *post* initial route.

Pattern:

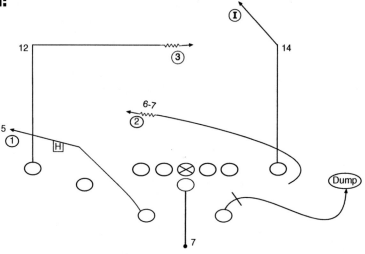

Quarterback Drop Timing: Seven steps.

Key Thoughts: Quarterback takes the initial read of the tight end's *post* route, if there. Quarterback then reads tailback's *flat* route to flanker's *shallow* route to split end's *cross*. Fullback's *swing* route can act as the dump-off route.

Alternate Pattern Application:

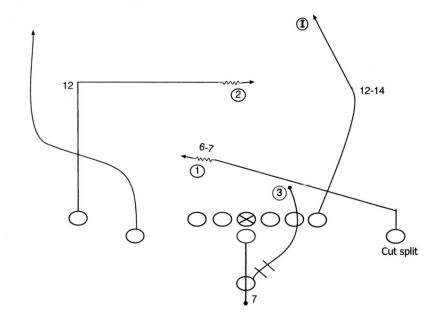

70. TIGHT END/SLOT SHALLOW CROSS

Concept: Seven-step, timed double *shallow* cross pattern with a *post* initial read route backside. Most effective vs. man coverages.

Pattern:

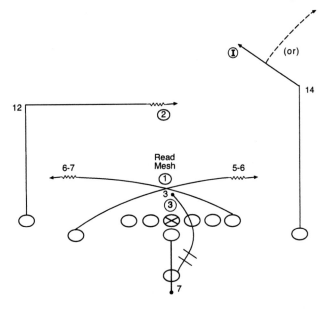

Quarterback Drop Timing: Seven steps.

Key Thoughts: Quarterback takes the initial read of the flanker's *post* route, if there. Quarterback then reads the mesh of the two crossing *shallow* routes to see if one comes open. If not, quarterback looks for split end's *cross* route to back's *middle dump*.

Alternate Pattern Application: From trips set.

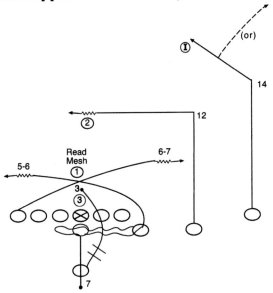

71. DOUBLE TIGHT END SHALLOW CROSS

Concept: Seven-step, timed double *shallow* cross pattern with a *post* initial read route backside. Most effective vs. man coverages.

Pattern:

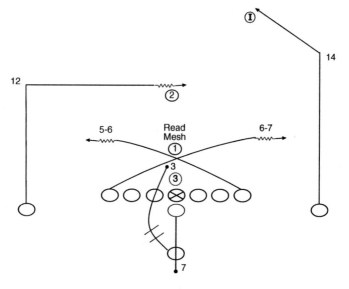

Quarterback Drop Timing: Seven steps.

Key Thoughts: Quarterback takes the initial read of the flanker's *post* route, if there. Quarterback then reads the mesh of the two crossing *shallow* routes to see if one comes open. If not, quarterback looks for split end's *cross* route to back's *middle-dump*.

Alternate Pattern Application: Double *cross*, double *post*.

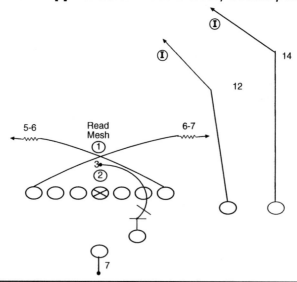

92

72. TIGHT END/SPLIT END SHALLOW CROSS

Concept: Seven-step, timed double *shallow* cross pattern. Most effective vs. man coverages.

Pattern:

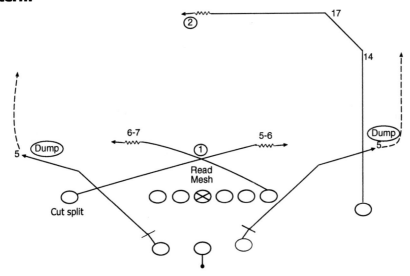

Quarterback Drop Timing: Seven steps.

Key Thoughts: Quarterback reads the mesh of the two crossing *shallow* routes to see if one comes open. If not, quarterback looks for flanker's *dig* route. Back's *flat* routes can be used as dump-off routes.

Alternate Pattern Application: From trips set.

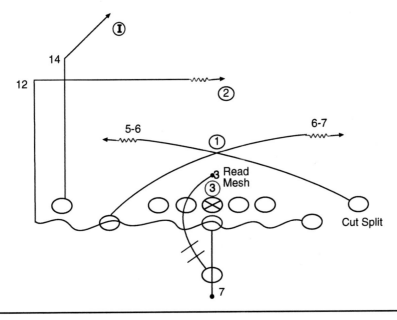

73. FLANKER/SPLIT END SHALLOW CROSS

Concept: Seven-step, double *shallow* cross pattern with tight end *post* initial read route. Most effective vs. man coverage.

Pattern:

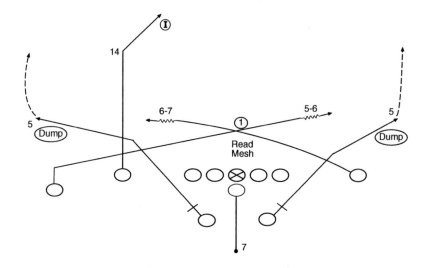

Quarterback Drop Timing: Seven steps.

Key Thoughts: Quarterback takes the initial read of the tight end's *post* route, if there. Quarterback then reads the mesh of the two crossing *shallow* routes to see if one comes open. Back's *flat* routes can act as a dump-off routes.

Alternate Pattern Application:

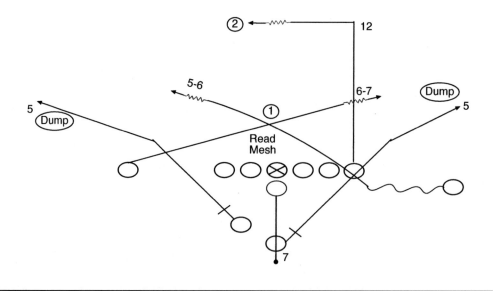

74. SLOT SHALLOW FOLLOW

Concept: Five-step, timed inside, inside-out scan pattern with a backside seven-step timed outlet.

Pattern:

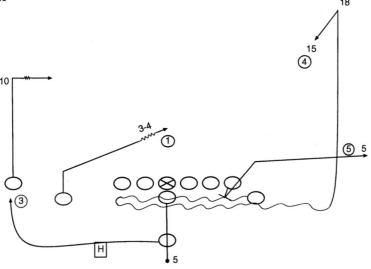

Quarterback Drop Timing: Five steps.

Key Thoughts: Quarterback reads slot's *shallow* route to split end's *curl* route to back's *swing*. The backside *hook/flat* route combination is the outlet (reading *hook* outlet first).

Alternate Pattern Application:

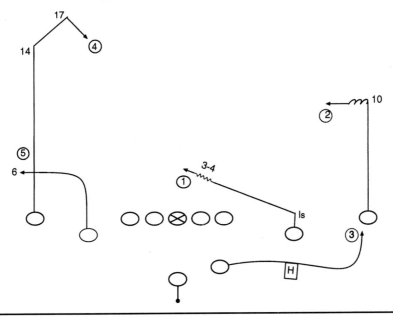

75. SPLIT END SHALLOW FOLLOW SWITCH

Concept: Five-step, timed inside-out scan pattern with a seven-step timed outlet backside.

Pattern:

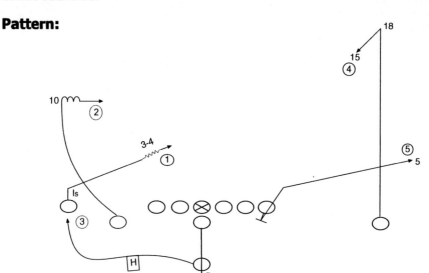

Quarterback Drop Timing: Five steps.

Key Thoughts: Quarterback reads split end's *shallow* route to slot's *switched curl* route to back's *swing*. The backside *hook/flat* route combination is the outlet (reading *hook* outlet first).

Alternate Pattern Application:

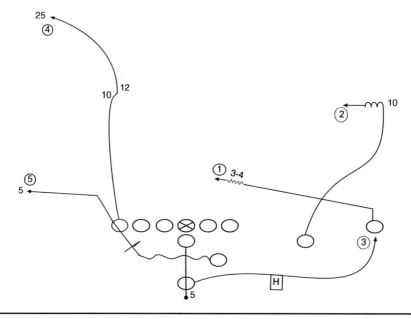

76. FLANKER SHALLOW TIGHT END FOLLOW

Concept: Five-to-seven step, timed across the field scan pattern with quarterback scanning back to outlets working into the quarterback's scan vision.

Pattern:

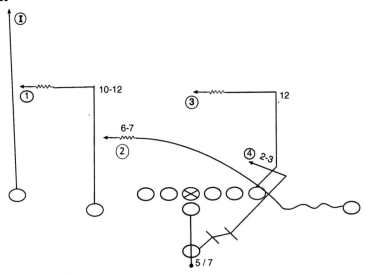

Quarterback Drop Timing: Five steps.

Key Thoughts: Quarterback has time to check outside initial *streak* route. Quarterback scans from slot's *square-out* route to flanker's *shallow* to tight end's *cross* route to back's *delayed-cross*.

Alternate Pattern Application:

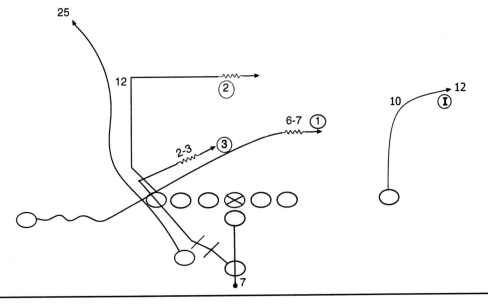

77. TIGHT END SHALLOW DOUBLE FOLLOW

Concept: Five-to-seven step, timed across the field scan pattern with quarterback scanning back to outlets working into the quarterback's scan vision.

Pattern:

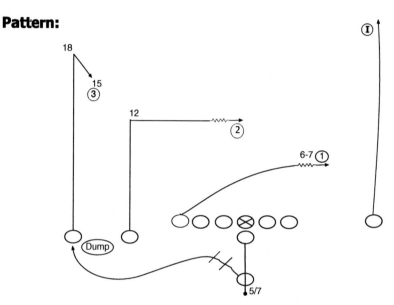

Quarterback Drop Timing: Five-to-seven steps.

Key Thoughts: Quarterback has time to look at the split end's *streak* initial read route before going to the tight end's *shallow* route. Quarterback then scans to slot's *cross* route to flanker's *hook*. The back's *swing* route is the dump-off outlet.

Alternate Pattern Application: Tight end's *shallow*, flanker's *layer*.

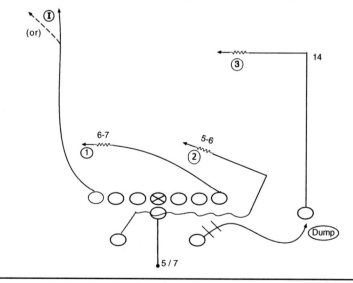

78. SLOT SHALLOW DOUBLE FOLLOW

Concept: Five-to-seven step, timed across the field scan pattern with quarterback scanning back to outlets working into the quarterback's scan vision.

Pattern:

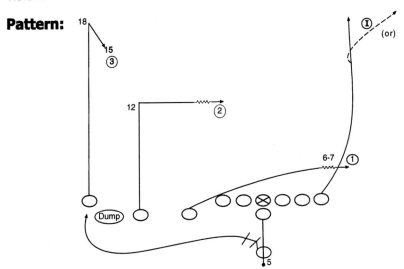

Quarterback Drop Timing: Five-to-seven steps.

Key Thoughts: Quarterback has time to look at the tight end's *streak* (or *flag*) initial read route. Quarterback then scans to slot's *shallow* route to flanker-slot's *cross* route to the split end's *hook*. The back's *swing* route is the dump-off outlet.

Alternate Pattern Application: With wing motion.

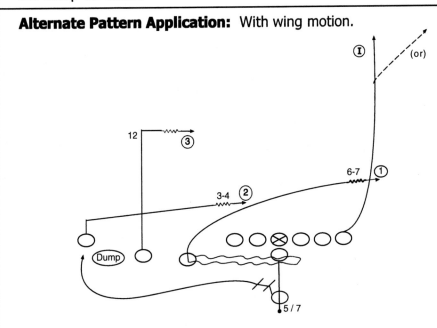

79. TIGHT END FLAG SPLIT END SHALLOW

Concept: Seven-step, timed flood pattern.

Pattern:

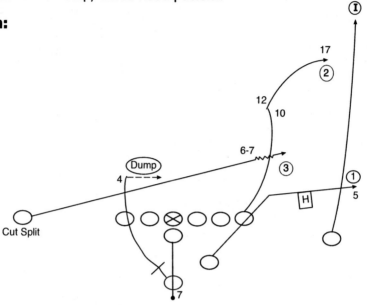

Quarterback Drop Timing: Seven steps.

Key Thoughts: Quarterback reads halfback's *flat* route to tight end's *flag* route to split end's *shallow* route. The fullback's *dump* route is the outlet.

Alternate Pattern Application:

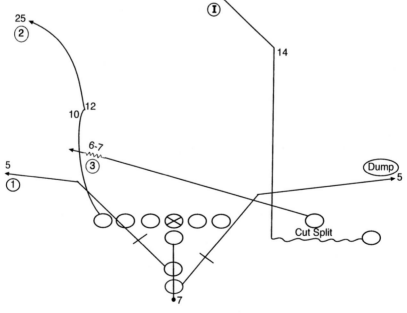

100

80. TIGHT END SMASH SPLIT END SHALLOW

Concept: Seven-step, timed flood pattern with back's *streak* initial read route.

Pattern:

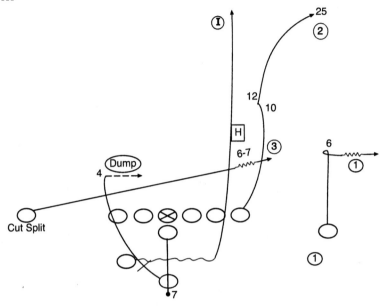

Quarterback Drop Timing: Seven steps.

Key Thoughts: Quarterback sneaks a peek at fullback's *streak* route before sequencing from flanker's *smash* route to tight end's *flag* route to split end's *shallow*.

Alternate Pattern Application:

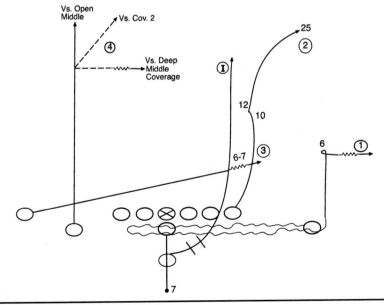

81. TIGHT END FLAG FLANKER SHALLOW

Concept: Seven-step, timed flood pattern with a backside *post* initial read route.

Pattern:

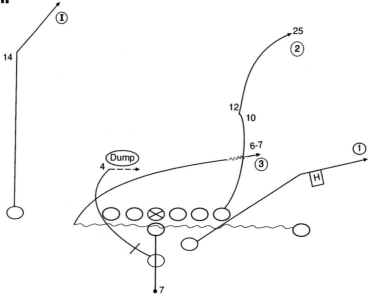

Quarterback Drop Timing: Seven steps.

Key Thoughts: Quarterback takes the initial read route of the split end's *post* route, if there. Quarterback then sequences from halfback's *flat* route to the tight end's *flag* route to the flanker-slot's *shallow* route. The fullback's *dump* route serves as the outlet.

Alternate Pattern Application:

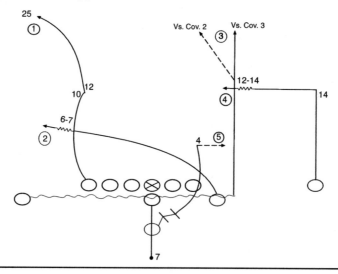

CHAPTER 9

FLAG PATTERNS

82. TIGHT END FLAG Z PIVOT

Concept: Five-step, timed flood pattern with a backside seven-step timed outlet.

Pattern:

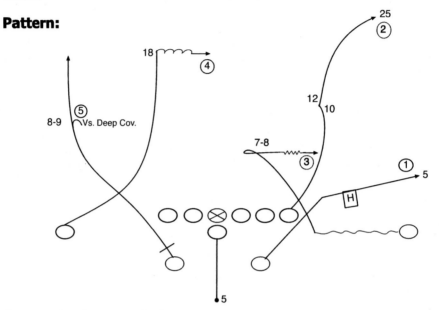

Quarterback Drop Timing: Five steps.

Key Thoughts: Quarterback reads fullback's *flat* route and then scans to tight end's *flag* route to flanker's *pivot*. Quarterback then scans to backside for *hook/wheel* outlet.

Alternate Pattern Application: Slot's *flag*, split end's *pivot*.

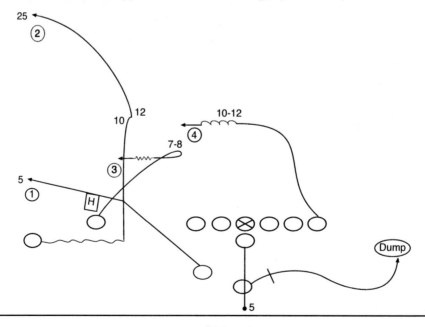

83. TIGHT END FLAG FLANKER SQUARE IN

Concept: Five-step, timed flood pattern with a backside seven-step, timed outlet.

Pattern:

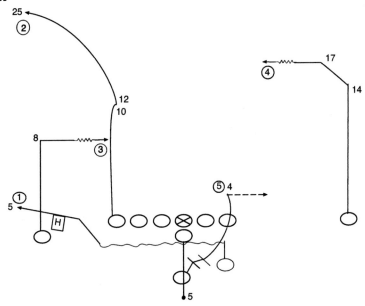

Quarterback Drop Timing: Five steps.

Key Thoughts: Quarterback reads tailback's *flat* route and scans to tight end's *flag* route to flanker's *quick square-in*. Quarterback then scans backside to *dig/dump* outlet route combination.

Alternate Pattern Application: Tight end's *flag*, flanker's *delay*.

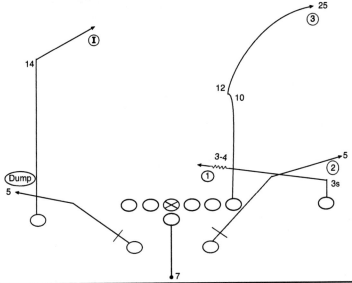

84. SLOT FLAG SPLIT END SQUARE IN

Concept: Five-step, timed flood pattern with backside *flag* initial read route.

Pattern:

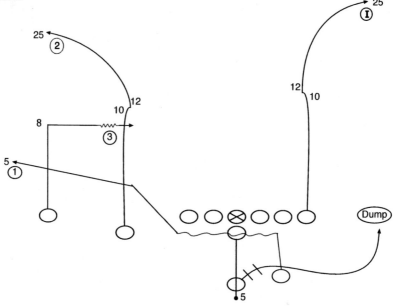

Quarterback Drop Timing: Five steps.

Key Thoughts: Quarterback takes the initial read route of the tight end's *flag* route, if there. Quarterback then sequences halfback's *flat* route to slot's *post-corner* to split end's *quick square-in*.

Alternate Pattern Application:

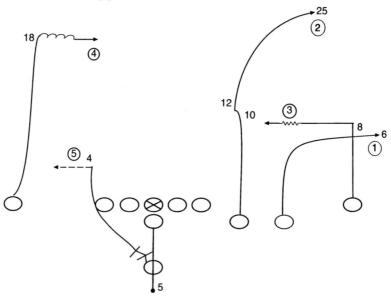

106

85. FULLBACK FLAG FLANKER WHEEL OUT

Concept: Seven-step, timed flood pattern with a backside seven-step, timed outlet.

Pattern:

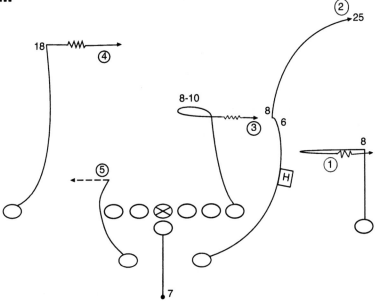

Quarterback Drop Timing: Seven steps.

Key Thoughts: Quarterback read flanker's *wheel-out* route and scans to fullback's *flag* route to tight end's *pivot-out*. Quarterback then scans backside to *dig/dump* combination for outlet.

Alternate Pattern Application:

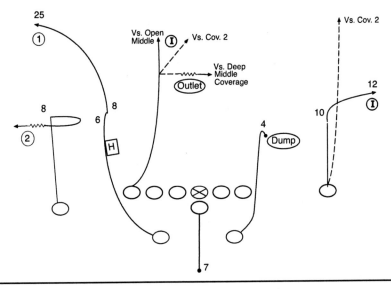

86. FULLBACK FLAG WING SHALLOW

Concept: Seven-step, timed flood pattern with a *post* initial read route and a backside seven-step, timed outlet.

Pattern:

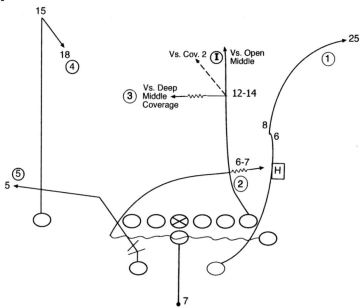

Quarterback Drop Timing: Seven steps.

Key Thoughts: Quarterback takes the initial read route of the tight end's *post* route, if there. Quarterback reads fullback's *flag* to wing's *shallow* route. Quarterback then scans backside to *hook* route as outlet.

Alternate Pattern Application: Fullback's *flag*, halfback's *flat*.

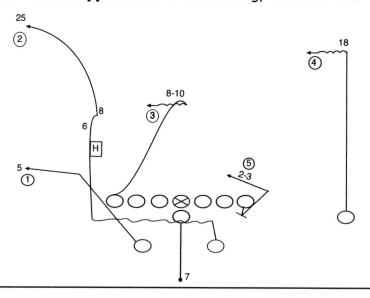

87. FULLBACK FLAG TIGHT END UNDER

Concept: Seven-step, timed flood/crossing route combination with a backside seven-step, timed outlet.

Pattern:

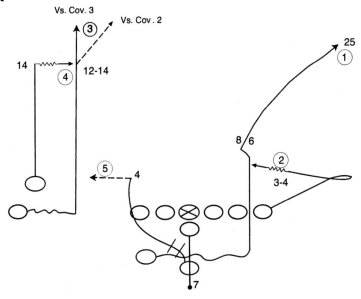

Quarterback Drop Timing: Seven steps.

Key Thoughts: Quarterback reads halfback's *flag* route and sequences down to tight end's *under* route. Quarterback then scans backside to flanker-slot's *streak/post* route to split end's *dig*.

Alternate Pattern Application: Fullback's *flag*, tight end's *wheel out*.

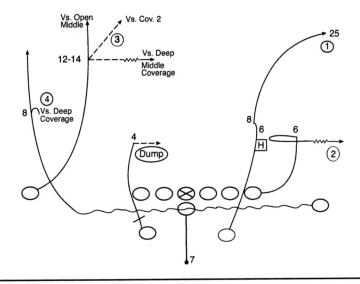

88. FULLBACK FLAG FLANKER PIVOT INSIDE

Concept: Five-step, timed flood pattern with a *post* initial read route and a backside seven-step, timed outlet.

Pattern:

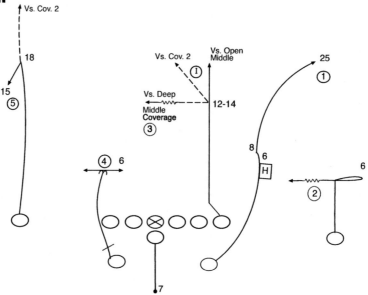

Quarterback Drop Timing: Five-to-seven steps.

Key Thoughts: Quarterback takes the initial read route of the tight end's *post* route, if there. Quarterback reads fullback's *flag* route to flanker's *pivot-in*. Quarterback scans to tight end's hook-up possibility to back's *option* route to split end's *comeback out* route for outlets.

Alternate Pattern Application:

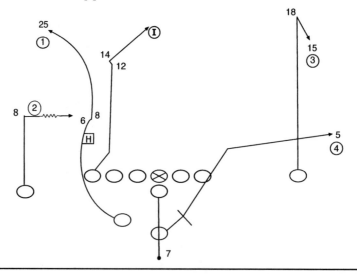

89. FULLBACK FLAG FLOOD

Concept: Seven-step, timed flood pattern with backside seven-step, timed outlet.

Pattern:

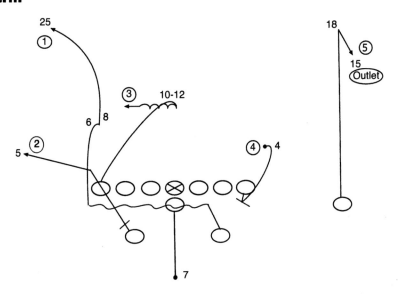

Quarterback Drop Timing: Seven steps.

Key Thoughts: Quarterback reads halfback's *flag* route and sequences down to fullback's *flat* route. Quarterback then scans to tight end's *middle hook/pivot* to backside tight end's *dump* to flanker's *comeback out*.

Alternate Pattern Application: Tailback's *flag flood*.

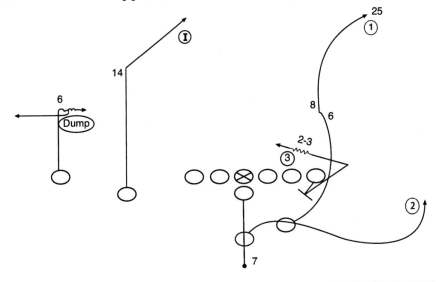

CHAPTER 10

TRIPS PATTERNS

90. TRIPS FLOOD

Concept: Seven-step, timed three-tiered flood route pattern with a backside outlet.

Pattern:

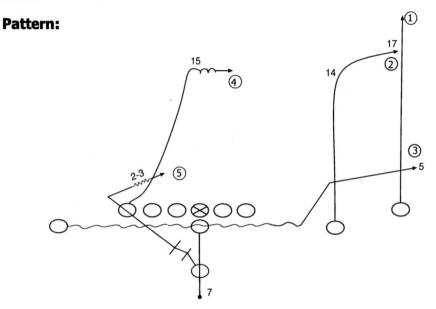

Quarterback Drop Timing: Seven steps.

Key Thoughts: Quarterback reads *streak* route deep which enables the quarterback to see the flood *flag* route of the flanker-slot underneath. The inside slot's *flat* route is the third read. The *middle-hook* route of the tight end and the back's delayed *scissor* route are the outlets.

Alternate Pattern Application: With inside-slot running *flag flood* route.

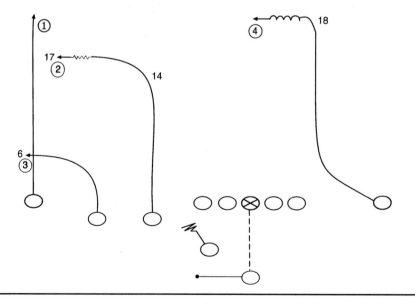

91. TRIPS HOOK CLEAR

Concept: Seven-step, timed lateral read *hook* pattern with a backside outlet.

Pattern:

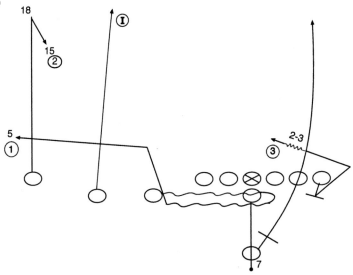

Quarterback Drop Timing: Seven steps.

Key Thoughts: Quarterback throws slot's *flat* route until he can't, unless deeper yardage is needed. *Flat* coverage means an opening up of the *hook*. Quarterback scans to the tight end's *delay* route as the outlet.

Alternate Pattern Application: With flanker-slot running *quick-out*.

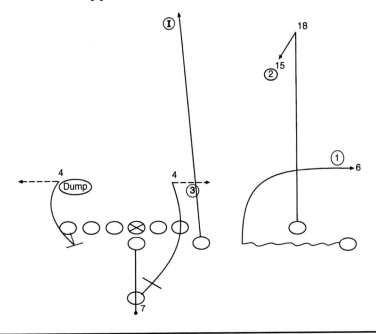

92. TRIPS FOUR-STREAKS

Concept: Five-step, timed four-*streaks* pattern from a trips set in an attempt to create a 2-on-1 *streak* isolation or a possible outside 1-on-1 *streak* isolation.

Pattern:

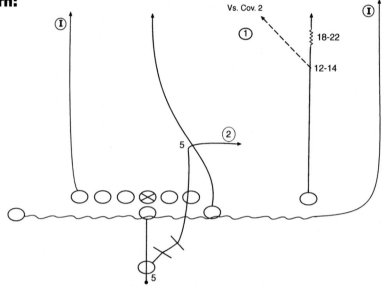

Quarterback Drop Timing: Five steps.

Key Thoughts: Quarterback looks for inside 2-on-1 *streak* isolation vs. a single safety. If two-deep, read split end's *post* break. Quarterback should still initially check for a good outside 1-on-1 *streak* isolation throw. If playside linebacker drops underneath *post* route, quarterback should come down to back's *dump* route.

Alternate Pattern Application: With back's *streak*.

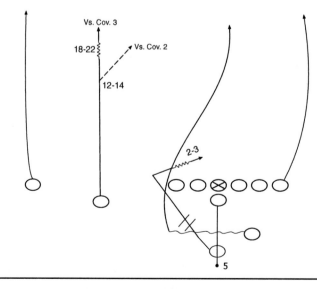

116

93. TRIPS POST-CORNER DOUBLE POST

Concept: Seven-step, timed weak flood pattern from a trips formation in an attempt to create a 3-on-2 deep isolation.

Pattern:

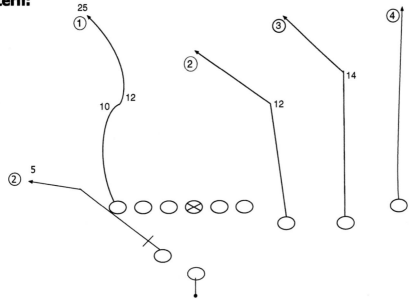

Quarterback Drop Timing: Seven steps.

Key Thoughts: Quarterback high/low reads for possible tight end's *post-corner* route throw or to the back's *flat*. If "color" appears on the *post-corner* from over the top, quarterback scans to slot's *short post* to flanker-slot's *deep post*.

Alternate Pattern Application: With flanker's *shallow*.

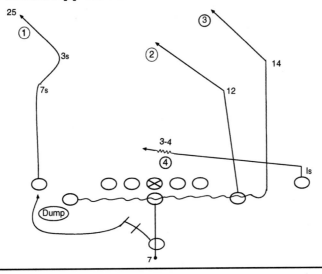

94. TRIPS SMASH

Concept: Seven-step, timed *post-corner/smash* flood pattern to create both high/low and flood read isolations with a backside tight end's *post* initial read route.

Pattern:

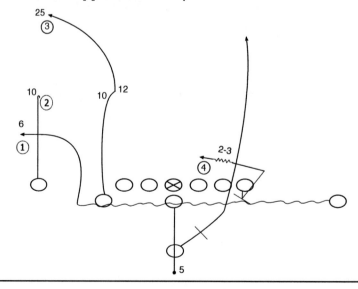

Quarterback Drop Timing: Seven steps.

Key Thoughts: Quarterback takes the initial read route of the tight end's *post*, if there. Quarterback then high/low reads. When in double, throw low. Never throw over the head of a retreating defender. Scan inside to slot's *post wheel-out* route for outlet.

Alternate Pattern Application: Trips *smash curl flat.*

95. TRIPS SMASH-MIDDLE READ

Concept: Five-to-seven step, timed middle-read/high-low read *smash* pattern. Best used vs. a two-deep coverage.

Pattern:

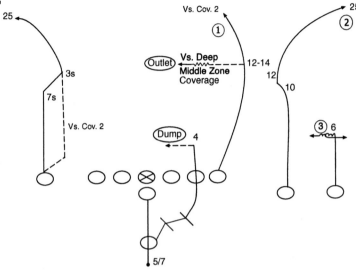

Quarterback Drop Timing: Five-to-seven steps.

Key Thoughts: Versus two-deep middle, quarterback looks to throw a five-step, timed tight end *post* route and then works outside to high/low *post-corner/smash* route combination of the slot and flanker. The tight end *square-in* adjustment action vs. a three-deep middle and the back's *dump* routes are the outlets.

Alternate Pattern Application: Trips wing *middle-read*, tight end's *pivot*.

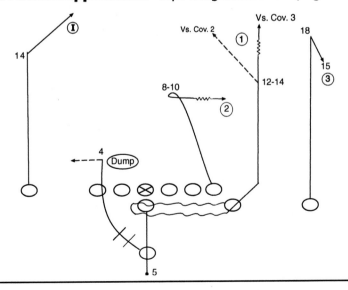

96. TRIPS TIGHT END OPTION

Concept: A three-to-five step, timed tight end's *option* route with a slot *speed-out* route frontside to control blitz and a backside *post* initial read route.

Pattern:

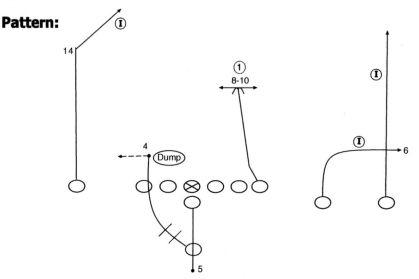

Quarterback Drop Timing: Three-to-five steps.

Key Thoughts: Quarterback takes the initial read of the split end's *post* route, if there. Quarterback then checks flanker's *fade*/slot's *speed-out* combination to combat blitz or if coverage gives a clean *speed-out* throw. Quarterback then takes tight end's *option*. The back's *dump* route weak is the outlet.

Alternate Pattern Application: Trips slot option.

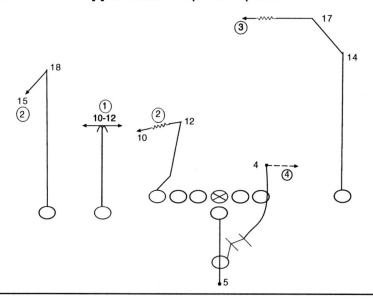

CHAPTER 11

BUNCH PATTERNS

97. BUNCH PIVOT

Concept: Five-step, timed bunched flood pattern with a backside seven-step, timed outlet.

Pattern:

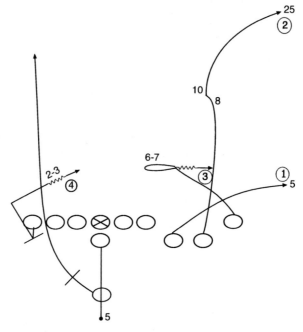

Quarterback Drop Timing: Five steps.

Key Thoughts: Quarterback reads inside slot's *flat* route and scans to flanker-slot's *post-corner* route to split end's *pivot*. Quarterback then scans backside to tight end's *delay* route as outlet.

Alternate Pattern Application: Bunch *pivot stop*.

98. BUNCH PIVOT CURL

Concept: Five-step, timed bunched flood pattern.

Pattern:

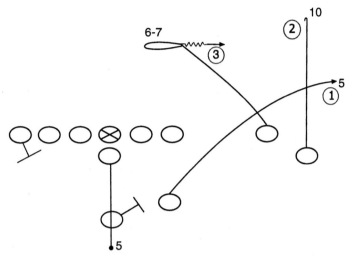

Quarterback Drop Timing: Five steps.

Key Thoughts: Quarterback read the halfback's *flat* route and scans to the flanker's *stop-hook* route to the split end's *pivot*.

Alternate Pattern Application: Bunch *pivot smash*.

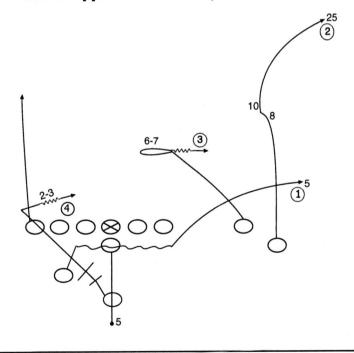

99. BUNCH SMASH

Concept: Five-step, timed bunched *post-corner/smash* pattern to create a high/low read isolation with a *post* initial read route.

Pattern:

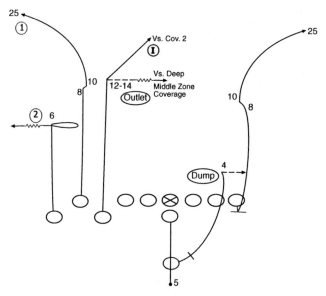

Quarterback Drop Timing: Five steps.

Key Thoughts: Quarterback takes the initial read of the inside slot's *post* route, if there. Quarterback then high/low reads the corner. When in doubt, the quarterback should throw low. Never throw over the head of a retreating defender. The tight end's *square-in* adjustment vs. a three deep middle and the back's *dump* route are the outlets.

Alternate Pattern Application: Bunch *smash stop*.

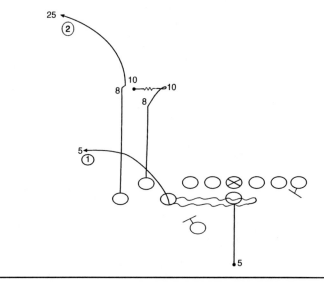

100. BUNCH OPTION SMASH

Concept: Five-to-seven step, timed bunched *option* and high/low *post-corner/smash* pattern with backside *deep tight end scat* route outlet.

Pattern:

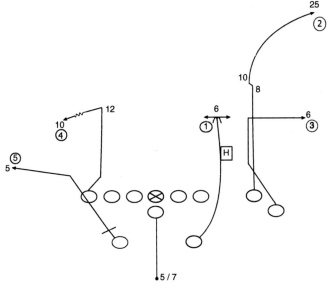

Quarterback Drop Timing: Five-to-seven steps.

Key Thoughts: Quarterback reads the halfback's *option* route and scans high to split end's *post-corner* route to low to the flanker's *short square-out* route. The backside tight end's *deep scat* route is the outlet.

Alternate Pattern Application: Bunch *smash pivot.*

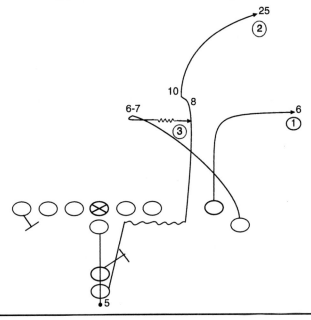

101. BUNCH SPLIT END ISOLATION

Concept: Five-or-seven step, timed split end isolation with quarterback scanning back to outlets working into the quarterback's scan vision.

Pattern:

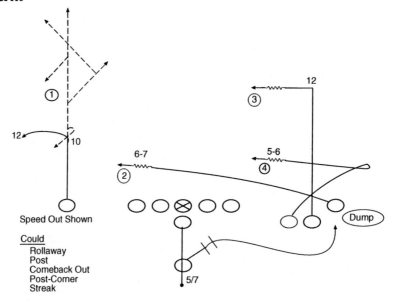

Quarterback Drop Timing: Five-or-seven steps (depending on split end's isolation).

Key Thoughts: Quarterback looks to throw the called five- or seven-step, timed split end prime route. Quarterback then scans back to flanker's *shallow* route to tight end's *cross* route to inside slot's *under-cross*. The back's *swing* route is the dump outlet.

Alternate Pattern Application: Bunch *double cross.*

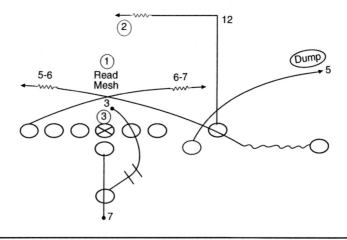

ABOUT THE AUTHOR

Steve Axman is an assistant coach on the University of Washington's staff. After coaching the Husky quarterbacks in 1999, he then added the responsibilities as the assistant head coach and wide receivers coach in 2000. As quarterbacks coach, Axman oversaw the work of Husky quarterback Marques Tuiasosopo, who finished his outstanding career by being named the Pac-10 Offensive Player of the Year and then the MVP of the Rose Bowl. In 1999, Axman's first year at the UW, Tuiasosopo led the Pac-10 in total offense and became the first quarterback in NCAA history to rush for 200 yards and pass for 300 yards in one game.

Axman is no stranger to West Coast football or producing top-flight collegiate quarterbacks. Among his former collegiate pupils are Troy Aikman (UCLA), Neil O'Donnell (Maryland) and Jeff Lewis (Northern Arizona). Washington is the fourth Pac-10 school where Axman has worked as an assistant coach. He joined the Husky program after serving as the quarterbacks coach at Minnesota in 1998 under Glen Mason.

Prior to joining the Golden Gophers' staff, Axman was the head coach at Northern Arizona from 1990-97. He inherited a NAU program that had experienced just three winning seasons during the 1980s and had never qualified for the Division I-AA postseason playoffs. During his eight years with the Lumberjacks, Axman guided the team to a 48-41 record, making him the second-winningest coach in Northern Arizona's history.

Axman's NAU teams were known for their offensive fireworks. During his eight-year career, Axman's teams averaged 30 points per game. His 1996 Lumberjack squad set or tied 14 national records and averaged 43.2 points per game en route to a 9-3 overall record and a 6-1 record in the Big Sky Conference. That season produced a second-place finish in the Big Sky, the school's first postseason appearance, and a school-best No. 6 national ranking.

In 1989, Axman served as Maryland's quarterbacks coach where he worked with O'Donnell. He was the offensive coordinator at UCLA in 1987-88 where he coached Aikman. Prior to UCLA, Axman coached at Stanford (1986), with the Denver Gold of the United States Football League (1985), and at the University of Arizona (1980-84), as the offensive coordinator and quarterbacks coach. Axman previously spent a year at Illinois, three seasons at Army, and one season at Albany State. Prior to that, Axman's first collegiate coaching assignment was at East Stroudsburg

State in 1974. A 1969 graduate of C.W. Post in Greenvale, N.Y., Axman went on to earn his first master's degree from Long Island University in 1972 and his second in 1975 while coaching at East Stroudsburg State.

Axman has authored six instructional books on football. He has also been featured on seven well-received instructional videos on football. He is nationally renowned for his knowledge of offensive fundamentals, schemes, and techniques, particularly quarterback play.

A native of Huntington Station, N.Y., Axman and his wife, Dr. Marie Axman, an elementary school principal, have four daughters: Mary Beth, Jaclyn, Melissa and Kimberly.